METAL BLADE RECORDS INC.
5737 Kanan Rd #143 Agoura Hills, CA 91301-1601.
metalblade.com | youtube.com/metalbladerecords
twitter.com/metalblade | instagram.com/metalbladerecords | facebook.com/metalbladerecords

Visit us online at: **CannibalCorpse.net**

Jacket Art And Book Layout By: **Brian J Ames**

Jacket Photos By: **Alex Solca**

Album Covers By: **Vince Locke**

Photos By:
Alison Webster: Pages 12,14,15,16, 18 Bottom, 19, 24, 27, 28, 31, 40, 42, 47,
58, 60 Top, 61, 72, 74, 76, 78, 79 Bottom, 82, 84, 98, 103, 118 Bottom, 119 Bottom Left, 146-147, 151
Alex Solca: Pages 4, 20 Top, 20 Bottom, 30, 43, 81, 139 Top, 161
Alex Morgan Imaging: Page 8
Stephanie Cabral: Pages 41, 45, 60 Bottom, 77, 101, 124 Center
Alex Mcnight: Pages 44, 79 Top, 125 Bottom
Dave Hallett: Pages 59, 62, 63, 73, 80, 97, 100, 119 Right, 124 Bottom,
125 Top Left, 125 Top Right, 138 Top Left, 138 Center
Vince Edwards: Pages 96, 99, 130, 139
Eugene Vinogradov: Pages 75, 124 Top Right
Nick Erickson: Pages 118 Top Left, 119 Top, 138 Right
Susan Campbell: Page 124 Top Right
Jim Cookfair: Page 119 Center Left

Lyrics reprinted by permission Sony/ ATV Music Publishing and BMG Chrysalis

10   9   8   7   6   5   4   3   2   **1**

Bible Of Butchery

CANNIBAL CORPSE

The Official Biography

JOEL McIVER

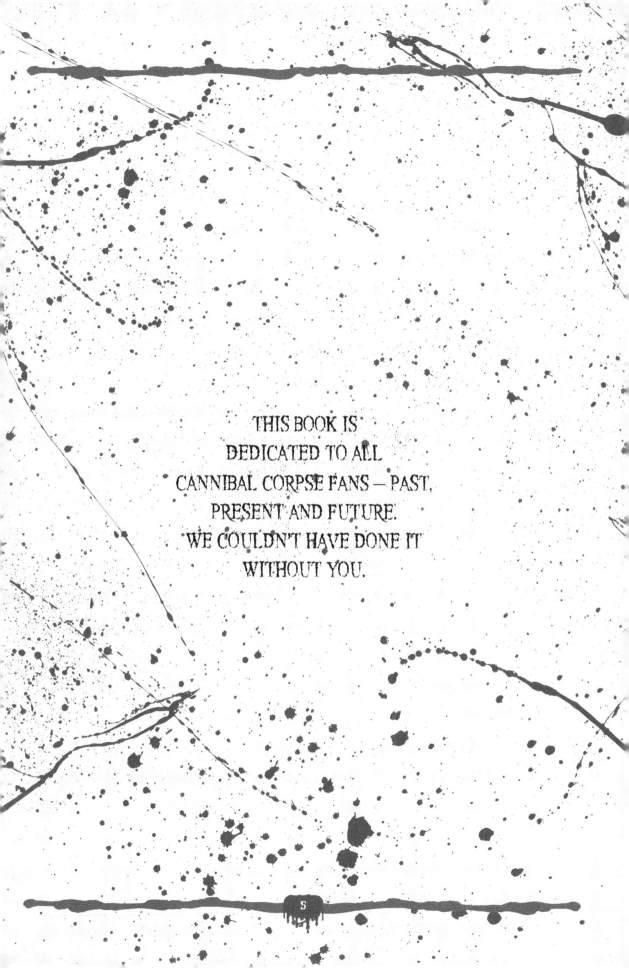

THIS BOOK IS
DEDICATED TO ALL
CANNIBAL CORPSE FANS — PAST,
PRESENT AND FUTURE.
WE COULDN'T HAVE DONE IT
WITHOUT YOU.

DISCLAIMER

This book is about the life and work of entirely normal people. The members of Cannibal Corpse are friendly, polite, fully house-trained musicians who have no nasty habits whatsoever, as far as the writer is aware. However, the lyrics of Cannibal Corpse's songs are not for the faint-hearted. Violence, torture, murder and many other disturbing practices are described in graphic detail. So don't read this book if you are sensitive, easily offended, or—in the case of minors—without the permission of your parents or guardians. Do not attempt to replicate any of the practices mentioned in Cannibal Corpse's songs. Any resemblance in said songs to any person living or dead is unintentional and entirely coincidental. You have been warned.

- Joel McIver, 2014

CONTENTS

The first time I met the members of Cannibal Corpse was in March 1989, when my band Dark Angel played with them at a venue called the River Rock Café in Buffalo, New York. This young band came up to us and told us that it was their first show ever. Cannibal were all really excited, because they liked Dark Angel and were really happy to be playing their first show with us. They had a friend named Mark "Psycho" Abramson, who has since had a very successful career working for Roadrunner Records, but at the time he was just the dude who worked with Cannibal Corpse. I met Mark recently when I was touring with Testament, and he told me that that one show kickstarted the entire Buffalo metal scene. There was literally no scene back then, but after that Cannibal Corpse had a following, which is extremely cool.

I've followed Cannibal's career closely in the 25 years since then. I remember when I saw their first record in 1990: I was like "Hey! That's that band whose first show we played at!" At that time, death metal wasn't quite what it became even a year later, and I have to admit that Cannibal's first couple of albums were a little noisy and a little hard to follow: it wasn't until the song 'Hammer Smashed Face' came out on the Tomb of the Mutilated album that they really caught my attention, because now they were starting to write really catchy riffs. That was so cool. When they put out The Bleeding, I thought that was an amazing record: it had awesome riffs all over it. In particular, the title song from that album is a monster.

I've always considered Cannibal Corpse to be a really aggressive thrash metal band as much as a death metal band, and I mean that as a real compliment. They've become the Motörhead of death metal, and again I mean that as a huge compliment, because whenever Motörhead plays a show, whether they have a new album out or not, it's gonna sell out, because it's an event and you want to go see them. Cannibal Corpse is the same: a lot of bands have lost their following over the years, but Cannibal hasn't, because they're a good band and they write killer metal songs. Their records are really tight, with an amazing production, and people get really stoked by them.

Alex Webster is an amazing bass player, and the musical focus of the band, which is great because very few metal bassists get much recognition apart from Steve DiGiorgio and a few others. He's played in project bands with some incredible musicians and he holds his own with any of them, which is a testament to his talent. Pat O'Brien is a great talent too: an awesome guitarist. It was great that he got to play with Slayer in 2012: what a great nod to the whole genre of death metal that was. Slayer could have gone with some known thrash metal guitarist, but they delved deeper and picked a guy from death metal. I remember when Nevermore toured with Death in 1995: Pat was playing with them then and I saw him wearing a Venom shirt on stage. He came to me and said, "I'm way more rooted in heavier music than this. Nevermore is a good band, and I like it, but if I get offered a gig with a heavier band, I'll take it." Sure enough, a couple of years later he was in Cannibal Corpse, and he's been a great fit ever since.

I remember when Strapping Young Lad played with Cannibal at the Busan Festival in Korea. Kreator were headlining, and the bill alternated between punk, pop and metal bands. When SYL started playing, to our surprise a ton of pyrotechnics detonated during the set. There was a light show, and sparklers, and flash pots and smoke going off throughout the set. I couldn't believe we weren't paying for all this stuff, as you normally do. Now, Cannibal went on after us—and they didn't want any of that happening in their set. They didn't want the crazy stuff. They said, "Just turn on some lights. Don't bother with the pyro. We're just gonna do our thing." They stuck to their guns and said, "That's not us." That is real self-confidence—and I respect that so much.

GENE HOGLAN, 2014

As I write this, it has been 26 years since the amazing Cannibal Corpse formed in Buffalo, New York, and 24 years since the Metal Blade record label signed them and issued their first album, Eaten Back to Life. On average, then, that's a quarter of a century that Cannibal have been in business—hence this book, written with the sole aim of celebrating their pulverizing career against all the odds, and published, appropriately enough, by Metal Blade.

You may have seen Cannibal Corpse's excellent DVDs, Centuries of Torment and Global Evisceration. If you haven't, make sure you do. The documentary footage on these releases covers the band's career in minute detail, raising the bar for any band considering a similar approach. This book chooses not to repeat that story for obvious reasons, complementing the DVDs with its own individual approach. Stack Bible of Butchery next to your Cannibal Corpse CD and DVD collection with pride: the focus that I and the band have maintained here is the personal histories of the band-members, the amazing photo archive that they and their fans have maintained over the years, and a comprehensive oral history, including a collection of slightly filthy on-the-road anecdotes that I persuaded the band to repeat with the aid of a blunt instrument.

I had a blast writing this book, from the first notes made in spring 2012 to these words, written in summer 2014. Most of my interviews with the band were executed over a few days which I spent on their tourbus as it traveled through the UK, in which time I got to know the musicians in a way that only being confined to a coffin-like metal tube can allow. While Cannibal Corpse's public image is uncompromising to say the least, in private these are relaxed, lucid, even cerebral people whose grasp of their mission is firm. They're out to deliver brutal music, of course, designed to enthral those—like you and me—who understand and appreciate it. But they're also out to be the best they can be, musically, lyrically and as a creative, functioning business entity. That's admirable.

Founder member Alex Webster is Cannibal's primary spokesman, a man who thinks before he speaks and who faces any criticism with disarming mellowness. Paul Mazurkiewicz, the other remaining founder member, is equally pleasant company, more excitable than Alex and as hyped-up as any extreme metal drummer needs to be. Guitarists Pat O'Brien and Rob Barrett are the quiet ones, the former a man permanently in search of a party and the latter more content with his own company and a good book. Perhaps Cannibal's biggest enigma is frontman George 'Corpsegrinder' Fisher, a mighty force on stage and a contemplative man off it: I recall on more than one occasion coming into the tourbus lounge at the dead of night, confronted by pitch darkness broken only a pool of light surrounding George's face, deep in thought while studying his phone, beer close at hand. These individual dynamics make Cannibal Corpse more than just the sum of its parts.

Now here's the part where I address not you, the reader who has been kind enough to buy, borrow or steal this book: I'm talking here to people who can't understand why the horrific nature of Cannibal Corpse's music deserves to be celebrated in book form, or in any form at all. Here's something I wrote when Cannibal's last album was released in 2012—and hopefully it will bring a little light to bear on the immense darkness that is their 13-album body of work to date...

"Cannibal Corpse's twelfth album in 24 years, Torture, is out in March, and as with all their releases, it's horrible. The album title sums up the songs' lyrical themes, an imaginatively obscene range of ways of being cruel to people. Torture deals in explicit detail with a series of experiences which most of us will never even imagine, let alone endure at first hand: 'The

Strangulation Chair,' 'Followed Home then Killed' and 'As Deep as the Knife Will Go' among them. The album is likely to sell rather well, and if their recent history is anything to go by, the members of Cannibal Corpse will take home a highly respectable income from the year-long tour cycle which follows.

"But why would anyone want to hear this depressing stuff, you may be asking? There's a simple answer, which is that Torture is breathtakingly good: an incredibly accomplished album

made by a band of great songwriting and performing talent. I won't try to convert you to the music, which is moderately technical death metal of immense speed and violence: you either respond to it or you don't. Most people don't, which is fine, but sufficient numbers of music consumers like Cannibal Corpse to have enabled the band, a quintet based in Florida, to make a comfortable living out of their albums and tours for the last two decades. No member of

Cannibal Corpse has ever had to flip a burger for money in that time. This is a claim that very few musicians can make, and—turning our perspective outwards—it's highly indicative of modern culture and the mindset of the people who populate it. The grisly tales which populate Cannibal Corpse's albums are all inspired by real life, which (as anyone who watches the news will know) is often a violent place to be.

"As Cannibal Corpse albums go, Torture is lightweight when it comes to graphic lyrics. The band have evolved away from the blunt shock/splatter approach that they took in their earlier years. Nowadays the horrors that they write about are more streamlined and precise, the equivalent of graduating from whacking a person on the head with a stick to dissecting someone with a scalpel. The initial line-up, which featured original singer Chris Barnes, wrote plenty of entry-level slasher stuff like 'Meat Hook Sodomy,' but also entered more challenging territory with 'Addicted to Vaginal Skin' and 'Entrails Ripped from a Virgin's Cunt.' The personification of the victims as female made the songs even more uneasy listening, naturally enough: what was even worse was when children became lyrical targets in the song 'Necropedophile.' This hadn't been done before (as far as this writer is aware) and the subject is still too much for most sane people, as the controversy which surrounded the similarly-themed A Serbian Film proved in 2010. Grim stuff, depending on how seriously you take it.

"Almost as depressing as the song themes is the regularity with which the members of Cannibal Corpse have been forced to explain that a) no, they don't take their violent lyrics seriously, b) no, they don't advise that anyone tries these things at home and c) no, they themselves are not violent or in any way generally extreme as human beings. Inevitably, people tended not to believe this in the first few years of the band's career, and indeed for some years Cannibal Corpse were banned from performing songs from their first three albums in Germany. The ban raised interesting questions about the nature of censorship, given that the vocals from Barnes and his successor Fisher are often unintelligible when sung live, and that few sensible people would give serious credence to such fantastically violent lyrics in the first place.

"The practicality of the ban was also debated: how would officials from the relevant government department enforce it? Would they demand to see the setlist for each show? How would they get into the venue anyway? Presumably not on the guest list, so would the relevant jobsworth be obliged to buy a ticket, thus supporting the very band they were trying to censor?

No-one was surprised when the ban was quietly lifted a few years ago—possibly, as the band-members surmised in interviews, because the relevant official was no longer in office.

"America has also had the occasional go at Cannibal Corpse, you'll be unsurprised to hear. When then-Senator Bob Dole said in 1995 that the band "undermined the character of the [American] nation," the group's profile benefited greatly. As it happened, the group's journey towards the

mainstream had taken an extra step the previous year, when Jim Carrey invited them to appear in his comedy Ace Ventura: Pet Detective. Now that Cannibal Corpse had appeared in a PG-13 film, who was offending whom, exactly?

"You'd be forgiven for assuming that songs such as 'Fucked with a Knife' and 'Stripped, Raped, and Strangled' came (at best) from spotty adolescent virgins or (at worst) violent psychopaths. The truth is that the members of Cannibal Corpse are neither: by and large, they are settled men in their forties with marriages, mortgages and families. They simply happen to be very good at telling horror stories that scare people because

they're about real people committing real atrocities, as opposed to those staple heavy metal inspirations, zombies and Satan.

"In fact, Cannibal Corpse's songwriters deserve a measure of respect for their imagination. After several albums of endless bloodletting, the songwriting has gone in some interesting directions – see 'Force Fed Broken Glass' and 'Bent Backwards And Broken,' both of which depict unusual ways of ruining someone's day. There's also a rich seam of humour behind some of the goriest material, although admittedly it's hidden deeply: any musicians who could write a song called 'Sanded Faceless' deserve a few free power-tool vouchers from Home Depot at the very least. The industrially-themed (in terms of lyrics, not music) 'Encased in Concrete' from the new album simply adds to the canon, one of the most relentless in the whole of music.

"These mesmerizingly aggressive songs may be unsettling, but they're as legitimate a form of entertainment as any other extreme expression of creativity, whether it's film, music or any version of the concrete and abstract arts. This is not to say that Cannibal Corpse's expert brand of death metal has to be analysed with an ironic eye, like some dickhead hipster who has just discovered his first HP Lovecraft novel. You're allowed to enjoy it. This is music which, if you so choose, will motivate you to leap off the sofa and climb the walls, shrieking like a fool. Or, if you prefer, turn the volume up to unsociable levels, sit back and immerse yourself in the annihilation of the senses, an all-enveloping perceptual blackout that resembles the flotation-tank experience in reverse. There's plenty of evil fun to be had here, so embrace it. Millions already have.

"But when it comes to the lyrics, it's really time for us all to grow up and stop being so offended. Who is responsible for the horrific events which inspire Cannibal Corpse's songwriting? Society itself, and it is you and I who make up society. You may be shocked by these songs, and rightly so—but there are real murders and real rapes aplenty out there out there in our lovely world. In comparison, such social ills reveal death metal's true nature as a form of entertainment. Violent entertainment, but entertainment nonetheless, and it's here to stay."

I can't find better words to explain why Cannibal Corpse matters than those. Read on, and you'll find exactly how it was that the musicians came together on their grisly mission in the first place.

JOEL MCIVER

PART 1:
MEET THE ACCUSED

GEORGE FISHER

THE LIFE AND TIMES OF DEATH METAL'S MOST INTIMIDATING
FRONTMAN. WARNING: FEATURES WORLD OF WARCRAFT.

I grew up in Baltimore, Maryland. I have a younger brother and a younger sister. My earliest memories? Let me think. I played baseball for a year or two in Little League. A local business called Flower Cart sponsored us and their name was on the back of our shirts. My mother still has the pictures.

I didn't really pay much attention at school, especially when I got into my teens and I just wanted to be in a band. I pretty much went to school because I had to. I could have learned, and I should have: I'd tell any kid to get an education. Learn as much as you can. But I just used to fuck around. I didn't want to hear what anybody wanted to tell me, because I just wanted to be in a band. I didn't graduate from my high school, Northern High School in Baltimore. My parents knew my heart wasn't in it. I wouldn't have listened even if they'd pushed me.

I heard Black Sabbath when I was fairly young, along with Accept and Iron Maiden and Judas Priest. Then later on, around 15 years old, I got into Slayer and Celtic Frost: a lot of different music came in about that point. Kreator were incredible. There were about eight to 12 of us who liked metal, but only me and one other guy who really got into the super-heavy stuff. I never learned to play an instrument, though. My mother bought me a bass, and I tripped over it and the headstock cracked, so I ended up selling it to someone and my mom yelled at me for that. I had a piece of a wood that my friends called the Rickenboarder—instead of Rickenbacker, right?— and years later me and Lee Harrison from Monstrosity did a demo called Sonic Vomit that had me on drums. I could play drums a little bit, I guess.

When me and some buddies were looking to form a band, which was difficult because there really weren't many people around who were into really heavy music, one of them told me "You need to sing because you know the lyrics to everything." That was true, although I didn't want to train my voice or anything. I don't have a singing voice anyway. I like listening to old country songs on the bus and I know I can't sing them, but I'll sing them anyway. I don't care. The other guys sit there and look at me. What I do in Cannibal Corpse isn't singing, though: it's growling, and it's not in key, although obviously I still need to know about timing.

Death metal growls came easily to me. In 1988, when my first band started, I was singing deep. Before that I used to practice singing in a death metal way. Death and Sacrifice were a big influences on me: the high screams I do definitely come from Chuck Schuldiner and Rob Urbinati. Slayer were huge for me too, and so was Tom G. Warrior from Celtic Frost. He wasn't singing as gutturally as, say, Jeff Becerra from Possessed, of course: those voices were more growly compared to the death metal singers of today. Later, in the 90s, I really liked Glen Benton from Deicide's vocal style, and John Tardy from Obituary as well.

My first band was Corpsegrinder; hence my nickname. I wasn't called that while I was in that band, only after I went down to Florida to cofound Monstrosity. Corpsegrinder played a lot of different stuff. It was just buddies of mine, really: we had two guitar players and we didn't have a bass player for years. We recorded a few things though, with me singing. We did that and went to local shows and talked to everyone we met about joining a band, but we never found anyone who was interested.

I went to a lot of metal shows. I'd go see Vio-Lence or Testament and people would come up to me afterwards and say, "You were the headbangingest person there!" But that's my philosophy: I think you should be completely brutal on stage. If you watch me on stage, you'll see I'm always either headbanging or singing, and there's nothing in between. Nobody else does that. It looks more savage that way. That's why I'm stationary on stage: I don't walk around much. You see some singers walk back to the drum riser and take a drink while rocking out with the drummer: I never do that unless I'm choking on something or whatever.

I don't really watch a lot of our shows back afterwards, by the way, because I don't like my talking voice. When I hear it I'm like, "Aaagh!", although I do like my singing voice. I never took any voice training lessons, though: I guess I just had a knack for mimicking a lot of guys.

Corpsegrinder played death metal mixed with hardcore: we weren't too serious, we'd drink and have fun and play metal. That happened when I met drummer Lee Harrison: we decided to form a band together.

Lee and I started working on putting Monstrosity together. I ended up being in that band for five years. There was a lot of partying going on, although I never did many drugs or anything, and there's a few things I don't remember. I used to talk with a deep voice on stage: I just thought you had to talk like that between the songs. I'll save all the Monstrosity stories for my own book. McIver ain't getting them.

Fast forward to Cannibal Corpse, who I'd gotten to know a little when I was in Florida. I already knew Rob Barrett from his band Solstice, and I think he probably pushed the Cannibal guys to get me when Chris Barnes left the band. I knew Alex Webster a bit too, we'd met at gigs. In fact, Rob and I were going to record some Celtic Frost songs: I was going to play drums and do vocals and he was going to play guitar and bass. For no reason, just for the fuck of it: just because we loved Celtic Frost.

Anyway, Alex called me up one afternoon in 1995 when I was at my mother's house in Maryland. I remember I was watching a football game and I'd just opened a beer. That's when he told me that they were kicking Barnes out. I was like, "Holy shit!" and told Alex to hang on for a second. I put the phone aside for a moment, maybe 20 seconds or so, and I had this feeling come over me that everything I had ever done up to this point was leading to this moment. He asked me if I wanted to come and try out, and I said that I would absolutely love to. He told me that they weren't trying any other singers out, but that they might do that later on if they weren't happy with me.

I was cool with that, because I knew the spot was mine, and that nobody was going to take it away from me. You see, I knew that if I played with Cannibal for one tour—just one single tour—I would deliver what they wanted, and it would be fucking amazing, or I would die trying. That was my mentality. You gotta have that attitude. I wanted to dominate every other band, and nobody was going to get in my way. Nobody.

I was like, "I'm gonna take this: I'm gonna show you motherfuckers that I belong here." I knew that any death metal kid who saw me with them would know that I was good. No fucking doubt about it. I have no animosity towards Barnes whatsoever, but the death metal singers that I respected were Chuck Schuldiner, Glen Benton, John Tardy and Dave Vincent. There are a lot of great singers out there. I think I have a pretty good voice, though. I can sing low, I can sing high, I can scream, I can go from low to high and high to low. I can do it all, I really can. I always believed that I was going to be in a big band and go somewhere. Not because I think I'm great or anything. I just always thought it would happen. Cannibal were already doing real well when I joined them, of course. I've never given up and I never will. If my back hurts or my neck hurts, I don't care: I'll fight through it. Same if I'm sick or hungover. As long as

my voice sounds good, I don't give a fuck.

So I went down there, and Cannibal had already been working on a new record, Created to Kill, which ultimately became Vile. I didn't try to replicate Barnes's vocals to please anybody: hell no. I do high stuff where he doesn't, and low stuff where he does. I knew that I would make people sing his songs the way I sing them—and they do. Does that make me better than him? That's not for me to say. But when you leave the show, you will leave thinking that I'm a maniac who headbangs like no-one else.

When we went and did the first tour, there were people in the crowd saying "Fuck you!" to me. That came with the territory. People still yell "Barnes!" now: they're trying to fuck with me. It's become part of the show for me to berate one fan and shout "I'm gonna kill your mother and make you drink her blood," and people laugh at it because they know I'm not going to do that. Now anyone who saw that from outside the circle of metal would be mortified if they saw that. They'd say, "That guy is fucking crazy!" It's all part of it.

You can't go on stage thinking, "I hope they like me." Fuck that. You can call me arrogant, and it's not the greatest quality to have in life, it's true—but if any kid asked me how to do what I do, I'd say "Don't have any fear. Don't be afraid of the crowd. Go on and do your thing—but know you belong there." It doesn't mean being a jerk to anyone after the show: there have been times when I've been exhausted afterwards and I tell people that I can't meet them but I'll see them next time we come up, because we tour so fucking much. That said, don't be a jerk. You do belong up there. As soon as the lights go down and you hear the crowd go "Yeahhh!", that's a feeling that's hard to replace. I get it every show.

On stage, I'm not a complicated person: I love headbanging, so I just do it. I watched Tom Araya do it when I was a kid, and it's not that complex. I wanted to headbang before I was in a band, and then I did it when I was in a band. It evolved, sure: I stood differently when I headbanged in Monstrosity and I went from point A to point B to point C.

I've always been a smartass on stage. A lot of people who came to see me in

Corpsegrinder were my friends, and they would be constantly breaking my balls when I was on stage, so I used to have to give shit back to them, which in hindsight probably helped with what I do now. Clarity is important, though. I try to enunciate song titles now so that everybody

will understand me, but I've seen people in the audience say to each other, "What did he say?" if I talk too much. Our guitar tech Bobby Binetti came up with the line about shooting blood out of your cock right before I announce the song "I Cum Blood." I wasn't saying much on stage at the time, and he said, "Come on man, say that!" and I was like, "That's fuckin' awesome."

There's always gonna be a debate about who is the best Cannibal singer. Do I want to win the debate? Fuck yes I do. I know Chris would want to win it too. I thank the fans for giving me the chance to prove myself. They could have all stayed at home and said, "Fuck you." But they proved that they like the band, not just the singer—which is fine with me.

A SKULL FULL OF MAGGOTS

LYRICS: BARNES · MUSIC: RUSAY, WEBSTER, OWEN, MAZURKIEWICZ

Lying there cold after a torturous death
Your life ended fast, you took your last breath
Dead in a grave, your final place
The maggots infest your disfigured face
Pus through your veins takes the place of blood
Decay sets in, bones begin to crack
Thrown six feet down left to rot
Brains oozing black down the side of your broken neck

Skull full of maggots

They enter your tomb
Maggots
Beginning to feast
Maggots
Crawling on you
Maggots
Now they eat you
Maggots
Rotting maggots
Maggots
Infesting your corpse
Maggots
Parasites of the dead
Maggots
Now dwell in your head

Lying there cold after a torturous death
Your life ended fast, you took your last breath
Dead in a grave, your final place
The maggots infest your disfigured face
Pus through your veins takes the place of blood
Decay sets in, bones begin to crack
Thrown six feet down left to rot
Brains oozing black down the side of your broken neck

SHREDDED HUMANS

LYRICS: BARNES, OWEN · MUSIC: RUSAY, WEBSTER, OWEN, MAZURKIEWICZ

Early hours, open road, family of five on their way home
Having enjoyed a day in the sun, their encounter with gore has just begun
A homicidal fool, not knowing left from right, now has the family in his sight
Trying to perceive if he's blind or insane
He steers his car into the other lane

Both of them collide, expressions horrified
Head on at full speed, the vultures will soon feed

The father of three was impaled on the wheel
As his skull became a part of the dash
His eyeballs ejected, his sight unaffected, he saw his own organs collapse
His seatbelt was useless for holding him back, it simply cut him in two
Legs were crushed, out leaked pus as his spinal cord took off and flew
The mother took flight through the glass, and ended up impaled on a sign
Her intestines stretched from the car down the road for a quarter of a mile

Fourth child on the way, won't live another day
Fetus on the road, with mangled little bones
Little children fly, not a chance to wonder why
Smashed against the ceiling, all their skin burning and peeling
Shards of glass explode, chest and skull now implode
Corpses they've become, and graves will have to be dug

Underneath the wheels, burning rubber on your face
Bleeding from your eyes, the slaughtered victim lies
Knowing what he's done, he just backs up one more time
Laughing at the mess, a pile of meat on the street

One child left slowly dying now, arteries gushing blood
Now it's time to feed on flesh, the gore has just begun

Early hours, open road, family of five on their way home
Having enjoyed a day in the sun, their encounter with gore has just begun
A homicidal fool, not knowing left from right, now has the family in his sight
Trying to perceive if he's blind or insane
He steers his car into the other lane

The look of death in my eye
Surely no-one will survive
Just a pile of mush
Left to dry in the sun

I see my fresh kill
Left in the road
Remains of your bodies
Mangled and torn

One child left slowly dying now, arteries gushing blood
Now it's time to feed on flesh, the gore has just begun

THE UNDEAD WILL FEAST

LYRICS: BARNES, WEBSTER · MUSIC: RUSAY, WEBSTER, OWEN, MAZURKIEWICZ

Undead feast, as they tear upon your weak flesh

Terror builds at the thought of being dead

Prophecy of the wise men of old

Now comes true, as the corpses break the soil

Ancient spell breaks the sleep of the dead

The dead awake, what the populace is fearing

Panic strikes as the nations run in fear

Oceans boil with blood of human victims

Suicide, the only way to avoid being eaten by the undead

Graveyards coming alive with zombies, hungry for living flesh

Psychotic, transmutated corpses, usurping the population

Sickening disaster of epidemic proportions, devouring us

Tables turn as a victim I've become now

State of death only waiting to return

Vital signs that show I'm dead

This can't happen, I'm rising from my own grave

Hunger grows, not nutritional but instinctual

Flesh becomes my only crave of this life

Unthinking state, a state of metamorphisis

Seeking food to keep me dead

Degenerate, a product of man's frustration for his error

Insatiable hunger for mankind, building with each kill

Seeking human victims to meet my fill

Cannibal I've become, what's happened to my brain

Feast on the corpse, suck out its brain

As its fluids drip down the drain

Chew on the bones, drink from its bladder

The vile stench only makes me madder

In through the mouth, out the forehead

Brains fall out, skin turns red

Violent surge, a spear through the skull

Felt the urge, now my heart's full

I crave gore, I'll eat your guts

I love gore, blood drives me nuts

I drink blood, I don't like water

Intestines my cud, I feast in the slaughter

Twist its neck, make it crack

Suicide, the only way to avoid being eaten by the undead

Graveyards coming alive with zombies, hungry for living flesh

Psychotic, transmutated corpses, usurping the population

Sickening disaster of epidemic proportions, devouring us

Blood I want to drink, I want to suck

Brains I want to eat, the rest I'll chuck

Bones into a spear, I'll carve and kill

Hunger for the quest, I'll never fill

I crave gore, I'll eat your guts

HAMMER SMASHED FACE

LYRICS: BARNES · MUSIC: RUSAY, WEBSTER, OWEN, MAZURKIEWICZ

There's something inside me
It's, it's coming out
I feel like killing you
Let loose of the anger, held back too long
My blood runs cold

Through my anatomy, dwells another being
Rooted in my cortex, a servant to its bidding
Brutality now becomes my appetite
Violence is now a way of life
The sledge's my tool to torture
As it pounds down on your forehead

Eyes bulging from their sockets
With every swing of my mallet
I smash your fucking head in, until brains seep in
Through the cracks, blood does leak
Distorted beauty, catastrophe
Steaming slop, splattered all over me

Lifeless body, slouching dead
Lecherous abcess, where you once had a head

Avoiding the prophecy of my newfound lust
You will never live again, soon your life will end
I'll see you die at my feet, eternally I smash your face
Facial bones collapse as I crack your skull in half

Crushing, cranial, contents

Draining the snot, I rip out the eyes
Squeezing them in my hands, nerves are incised
Peeling the flesh off the bottom of my weapon
Involuntarily pulpifying facial regions

Suffer, and then you die
Torture, pulverized

At one with my sixth sense, I feel free
To kill as I please, no-one can stop me

Created to kill, the carnage continues
Violently reshaping human facial tissue

Brutality becomes my appetite
Violence is now a way of life
The sledge's my tool to torture
As it pounds down on your forehead

ALEX WEBSTER

Right after we finished our first US tour, in support of the Butchered at Birth album, Paul and I got into an argument with Chris. We were unhappy with the way that certain things had been on the tour, although now I look back on it all these years later, none of it was a big deal. Paul and I quit the band for six or seven days. We talked to the guys who owned the rehearsal rooms and moved our stuff down the hall to a different room. We were literally about 50 feet away from the other guys.

So we started writing a new song, which was a very simple, pounding idea, at least during the introduction. We wrote a good chunk of it before we patched things up and got back with the other guys about a week later. They were happy to see that we had the start of a really good song. That intro reminds you of a hammer, and then there's that bass part, which the guitarists join in with. A lot of the solo bass parts came about because I wrote a riff and the other guys asked me to introduce it before they joined in. That little eight-note solo is made up of four different tritones. I'd been working on a lot of exercises at the time, and I was into Atheist and Cynic and I was trying to expand my bass playing, technically, by coming up with stuff that was a little more difficult to play and not in a key.

I might have come up with the title, although Chris did all the lyrics: I chose it because that simple intro sounds like somebody pounding on a nail with a hammer. It has a lot of pinch harmonics in it, which I'd heard a lot in Immolation songs and were a major influence on me. We also adopted octave chords into our sound, which had been pioneered by Morbid Angel.

I CUM BLOOD

Lyrics: Barnes · Music: Rusay, Webster, Owen, Mazurkiewicz

Swollen with liquid
Ready to burst
A load of my lymph
Will quench this dead body's thirst
One month in the grave
Twisted and half decayed
She turned a putrid yellow
I pissed in her maggot-filled asshole

Fucking the rotting
My semen is bleeding
The smell of decay
Seeps from her genital cavity

The smell was unbearable
As I unburied her
I cum blood from my erection
I feel it run down her throat, swallow
Eyes glassy and vacant
Body dug up to play with
Skin greasy and naked
Tonguing her rotted anus

I need a live woman to fill with my fluid
A delicate girl, to mutilate, fuck and kill
Her body exceptional
She thought I was normal but I wanted more

I came blood inside of her
Choking on the clot
Gagging on the snot
Gushing blood, from her mouth
Bloody gel leaking out
Body buried in a shallow grave
Unmarked for none to find
The sickness I have left behind
Undetected go my crimes
The greatest thrill of my life
To slit my own cock with a knife

Violent climax
Serging serum on my skin
Back from the dead
I am resurrected to spew putrefaction

was born in 1965 in Kentucky, in Covington, just south of Cincinnati. I have two younger brothers, one of whom is autistic. My childhood was good: I had a lot of fun, although I hated school. I couldn't wait to get the fuck out of there. I didn't feel I could identify with a lot of the people, especially when I was younger.

In high school I came a little bit more out of my shell, though. I smoked pot through most of high school, but I managed to graduate, largely because my parents wanted me to. They raised me to finish what I started. I played Little League baseball when I was younger, and I fuckin' hated it, but my mom said, "You have to finish this, because you made a commitment." It sucked, but I did it. My dad was a military man, and a ballbuster. He used to make me get up and jog a mile or two before school. When I was young he used to drink a lot, which was hard, but he quit when I was about 15.

The Beatles were my gateway to music. Any chance I got, I would listen to them, and one of the first albums I got was Peter Frampton's Frampton Comes Alive!, which I still think is a

good album. Then I got into rock bands like Pink Floyd and Queen, and I went on from there to Aerosmith— but when I discovered Black Sabbath, that was it. That was the band! I couldn't believe that this music existed, and that I'd been missing out on it. I didn't have a bigger brother to turn me on to this stuff, so I had to go and find it for myself. Someone gave me a copy of Sabbath's album Paranoid, that was the first album I got from them. I bought all their albums that were out at that time after that. Later, another friend gave me a copy of Sabbath's album Never Say Die! when it came out, so that would have been in 1978. I remember they came and played that same year at the Riverfront Coliseum with Van Halen, which was another band that I was into, and I wanted to go so bad, but my mother wouldn't let me because I was only 13. The following year there was a disaster at that same venue when the Who played: a bunch of people got stampeded. It was on the cover of Rolling Stone.

My aunt took me to see Cheap Trick, which was my first concert. I thought it sounded

like complete crap, because we were way up in the nosebleed section and the sound was messy, but there was something about it that was still cool. Then my mom bought me an acoustic guitar when I was 13: it had an action about an inch off the fretboard. I could barely play it, and I wanted an electric, but she told me I needed to learn on the acoustic first. So I started taking guitar lessons, learning Neil Young songs and stuff like that with basic chords. After a while I knew I'd gone as far as I could with it: I wanted to play some AC/DC songs. I liked them in the late 70s: I remember hearing that Bon Scott had died. It took me a while to accept Back in Black with the new singer. Typical metalhead mentality.

Then I really got into Judas Priest, because a buddy of mine kept talking about them. He said, "You don't know what you're missing, man!" so finally I went out and bought a couple of Priest albums. I listened to them and I liked the music straight away. I loved the heavy guitar sound, even in bands where the vocals sucked, so I learned to play a couple of the songs. Then I got into Iron Maiden and Accept: Restless and Wild was a life-changing album for me. It's one of the greatest heavy metal albums of all time, to this day.

When I was 15 I could finally get to some metal shows by myself, and as soon as I got out of high school I got a job teaching guitar. My first band was when I was 17, with friends of mine from school. We opened for Girlschool once, that was our biggest show. They were loud as fuck, it was just ungodly loud. Kelly Johnson, the guitar player, had two full Marshall stacks!

We were called Savatage, like the other band of the same name; in fact, when the better-known Savatage came out, that killed us off. We did some original songs but mostly it was covers. We broke up because of stupid shit, like all bands of that age do, and then I spent a couple of years playing in a covers band called Prizoner, which was a great way to become a better guitar player. I got my first road experience with that band, touring clubs in the Carolinas. It was exciting, but it was hard work.

I was a little bit obsessed with guitar tone in the early days: I'd try different guitar amps and really overthink the whole damn thing. I really liked the Stormtroopers Of Death guitar sound. In many ways their album Speak English or Die was pre-death metal. Prizoner actually opened up for Anthrax on the Spreading the Disease tour. That was pretty cool. But the covers band thing was limited: I'd see Metallica and Anthrax come out playing originals, and I knew that was the future. I wanted to do that, so I got out of Prizoner because I wanted to pursue my own thing and I knew I couldn't do it there.

I made friends with the guitarist David T. Chastain and wound up going on tour with him on the Seventh of Never tour. He used a couple of my riffs. I'd known him over the years because I used to play with my old band Savatage at a club near my house called the Round-Up Club. He'd been in a cover band called Spike, and was known as one of the best guitarists around. I used to watch him a lot and he was a big influence on me.

For a long time I was into AC/DC and Tony Iommi, so my first electric guitar was a cheap Gibson SG copy, just a cheap piece of junk called a Montoya. Then I was given a Gibson Les Paul and my dad bought me one of David Chastain's old Flying Vs, because I was really into Michael Schenker and UFO. I was into Randy Rhoads too, I saw him on the Diary of a Madman tour a few weeks before he died in March 1982. I play Vs as a tribute to my dad, because he came through and bought me my dream guitar.

It was hard finding musicians who could do what I wanted to do, although I wasn't quite sure what I wanted to do myself. I did know that I wanted to do something different and heavy, so I ended up hooking up with some guys in the band Ceremony, and I was able to finally get to a studio and record. Steve Tucker was the vocalist: he ended up joining Morbid Angel for a few years.

I also jammed with a band called Lethal around this time, who were signed to Metal Blade. They played in a kind of Queensryche or Maiden style. They never really got to tour, because their guitarist Eric Cook had health issues, but they had a show coming up and needed a second guitar player and so I filled in at a show. They wanted me to join them but I was focused on Ceremony at the time.

It took until 1991 to get anything recorded with Ceremony, though: it seemed like a long, long time. We got a demo done, but then we broke up due to some bullshit which I won't go into. A little piece of my heart stayed with that band, I have to say. But at least I had the demo, and Borivoj Krgin reviewed it in a column he wrote at the time. Machine Head's demo was on the same page, I recall.

Around this time I asked Borivoj if he knew any bands who needed a guitar player, because I was ready to leave, like, yesterday. He gave me Nevermore's address and I sent them a tape: I also sent one to Ozzy

Osbourne, who was looking for someone at the time as well. The Ozzy camp sent me a rejection letter but Jeff Loomis of Nevermore invited me up to try out.

I flew up to Seattle and landed the gig. I brought some of the heaviness from Ceremony into Nevermore, but Jeff Loomis is one of the greatest guitar players that I've ever been in the same room with. Watching him play was absolutely amazing. It was right after the grunge wave broke, so it was an annoying time for anyone who liked heavier music. It was a weird time.

I was with Nevermore for two years. I look back on it fondly in parts: it was hard being from Kentucky, which is the ass-end of the world, at least in America. If you say you're from Kentucky, people think you're a clueless son of a bitch and that you don't know anything. The prejudice probably wasn't there as much as I thought it was there, though.

I remember Nevermore's singer Warrel Dane saying to me when I arrived in Seattle, "Now you're in the big city" like I hadn't lived in a big city already. I knew about the tough side of life, actually, having lived near Cincinnati: I knew about drugs and crime and racial tensions, which are common there.

The relationship wasn't that good, sometimes. I felt like the odd guy out of the band and we didn't gel. It was probably my fault: I was drinking too much at the time. I wanted to do something heavier than Nevermore, and for that reason they let me go, paying me $500 for a whole tour. It was a little brutal, but I said "Fuck it, I'm out of here." I've never seen any money from the albums I played on with them. I didn't sign a contract with them, though, which was naive of me. That's why I don't trust people, because I'm sick of being naive and people telling me that everything's been taken care of—and you turn around and you're fucked.

So I moved to LA for a year. So now I was "Pat from Seattle." I was partying, hanging out on the beach and doing whatever odd jobs I could find, and just living for the moment. I had no direction and no purpose. The first month after arriving in L.A. was rough, because I thought I was done after Nevermore. I didn't have the energy to start a band from scratch. I even stopped playing the guitar for a while, but a few months later, a friend hooked me up with

Monstrosity, who needed a touring guitarist, and I went down to Florida and played with them for a tour. After that I started to have more fun. Life wasn't too bad after that. I liked playing with Monstrosity, but they were totally unstable as a band, and financially there was no way I could have moved down to Florida to join them full-time.

When Rob Barrett quit Cannibal Corpse in 1997, the slot came up for a guitarist. I went down there and learned the songs and played them with the band, but it was funny: they didn't tell me if I'd got the gig or not. I kept learning the songs and playing them with them, but they wouldn't tell me for the longest time if I was in or not! They were like "We're not sure" and then finally I said, "Have I got the gig or not?" and they told me I had. It was great to join them. I wanted that gig so badly. I was ready to give a lot more than I had in Nevermore, and also not to make the same mistakes. This time I was ready to give 100 percent and commit.

Cannibal had pretty much written the whole of Gallery of Suicide when I got there, apart from a couple of songs that they were working on. I had some ideas and came up with the music for "Stabbed in the Throat." They'd come up with the title and I wrote the song based on it. It was a real rush to finally write super-heavy songs at last. The vibe was totally different than it was in Nevermore.

I felt right at home in Cannibal Corpse. I was living with George in Temple Terrace in Tampa at first, because he needed a roommate, and then I moved in with Jack. That first year is pretty foggy because there was a lot of partying! I mended my ways in Cannibal, though: I decided that if I drank it was always going to be after the show, never before, otherwise I wouldn't be operating at my fullest. I was lucky to get into a second successful band, and this time I wanted to do it right, so I would go to the gym and then the rehearsal room, by myself, where I would write riffs.

In my downtime, I shoot guns. I've been interested in them since I was a kid. It's the other thing I'm interested in apart from guitars, and it's a great way to let off aggression. I go to ranges and shoot targets. Playing loud music is another good way to release stress. I like to go to the gym and work out, and I like to go out and drink and have fun with my buddies. Luckily, I've always been able to go anywhere and make friends. I live day by day. I would never have guessed that I'd still be doing this after all this time...

ADDICTED TO VAGINAL SKIN

LYRICS: BARNES · MUSIC: RUSAY, WEBSTER, OWEN, MAZURKIEWICZ

I don't know
I just took that knife
And I cut her from her neck down to her anus
And I cut out the vagina and I ate it

A relapse of my body
Sends my mind into multiple seizures
Psychologically a new human being
One that has never been

Cursed by the shaman
his voodoo spell has my soul
My limbs go numb
I can't control my own thought
Are his now
His evil consuming me
Ever telling me
Begin the clit carving

Slowly turning me, into a flesh-eating zombie
Knowing this spell can only be broken
By the vaginal skins of young women
I proceed to find the meat
Their bleeding cunts will set me free
I can't control my own thought
I can't control my own thoughts
Warmth seeping from this body
Rotted
After I sucked the blood from her ass

I feel more alive
More alive than I've ever been
Even though now I'm dead within

My mouth drools
As I slice your perineum
My body smeared
With the guts I've extracted
Through her hole, came swollen organs
Cunnilingus with the mutilated

My spirit returned from the dead
Released by the priest
But I felt more real when I was dead

The curse is broken
I have a dependence on vaginal skin
It's become my sexual addiction
I must slit, the twitching clit
Rotted cavity holds the juice

Between the legs, I love to carve
My cock is dripping with her blood

ENTRAILS RIPPED FROM A VIRGIN'S CUNT

LYRICS: BARNES · MUSIC: RUSAY, MAZURKIEWICZ, WEBSTER

Alive alone now that they've gone, dead but unburied
I've seen it unfold, terrible scenes of agony
Eyes in the darkness
Echoing their madness

The sights that have passed before them
Watching as though it has never happened
Now I only listen to what is not spoken

Murder, hatred
Anger, savage
Killings I have caused
More than can be counted
Orgies of sadism
And sexual perversion
Virgin
Tied to my mattress
Legs spread wide
Ruptured bowel, yanked
From her insides
Devirginized with my knife
Internally bleeding
Vagina, secreting
Her blood-wet pussy
I am eating
On her guts I am feeding
Mutilated with a machete
I fucked her dead body
The first and last
Your life's only romance
My knife's jammed in your ass
As you die you orgasm

Pass on to the dead
Nerve trembling convulsions
No longer looking human

I never see them, but I know they're there
Locked in my subconcious
Obscene memories I thought I'd forgotten
Haunting unrealities
Tear at me
Hold her arms
Her mouth taped shut
Screams unheard
Out pour her guts

Layers of flesh peeling away
Languish in your own decay
Descriptions of my killings
Bone chilling

Terror, tear, her
Virgin cunt

Virgins are my victims
Their tight interiors I explore
Sharpened utensils of torture
Now inserted inside of her
Sex organs extracted for eating
On her liver I am gnawing

Forbidden lust for guts
Ripped from her cunt
Tears of blood cry down her thigh

I ram my fist inside her hole
From her crotch piss now flows
Rectum filled with shit
I fucked her emptied body
Until she became stiff

FUCKED WITH A KNIFE

LYRICS BARNES · MUSIC WEBSTER

No escape from your fate

Destined to be mine

Every night I wait to see

In the night, watching

Stalking your every move

I know when you're alone

All alone

Tied tight to the bed

Legs spread open

Bruised flesh, lacerations

Skin stained with blood

I'm the only one you love

I feel her heart beating

my knife deep inside

Her crotch is bleeding

She liked the way it felt inside her

Fucking her, harder, harder

She liked the way it felt inside her

Fucking her, harder, harder

Stick it in

Rip the skin

Carve and twist

Torn flesh

From behind

I cut her crotch

In her ass I stuck my cock

Killing as I cum

ALEX WEBSTER

We really wanted to be fast on this one. Our songs have fast parts and slow parts: we wanted a tune that would be blazing fast all the way. No breakdown in the middle, or anything like that: just speed from beginning to end. The lyrics are suited to that. There's nothing subtle about Chris's lyrics here. It's everything you think it would be.

We never wanted any of our lyrics to be seen as funny: we want the listener to view each song as its own individual horror story, and they can be taken seriously in the way that a frightening horror movie can be taken seriously—but what we've found is that the gorier a song is, the more people inject a feeling of black humour into their interpretation of it. I can see that some of the songs are so over the top that you might find it amusing, but if you saw any of these things happening in real life, the last thing you'd be doing is laughing. You'd be trying to help the poor victim escape their predicament, or possibly running for your life.

The context adds that element of fun to something that is really morbid and macabre, and at a concert, we're having fun because we're playing really high-energy music and everyone's laughing and having a really good time. George will say some tongue-in-cheek funny stuff on stage when he's announcing the songs, and that helps lighten up something that's really quite dark, taken at face value. That's the way we design them to be.

As people we don't take ourselves seriously, but we do take our songs seriously—although of course we don't intend the lyrics to be any kind of instruction for living.

STRIPPED, RAPED AND STRANGLED

LYRICS: BARNES · MUSIC: WEBSTER, OWEN, BARRETT

They think they know who I am
All they know is I love to kill
Face down, dead on the ground
Find me before another is found

I come alive in the darkness
Left murdered and nameless
Dead unburied and rotten
Half eaten by insects

She was so beautiful
I had to kill her

Tied her up
And taped her mouth shut
Couldn't scream
Raped violently
Rope tight, around her throat
Her body twitches
As she chokes

Strangulation caused her death
Just like all the others
Raped before and after death
Stripped, naked, tortured

They're all dead, they're all dead
They're all dead, by strangulation

I come alive in the darkness
Left murdered and nameless
Dead unburied and rotten
Half eaten by insects

It felt so good to kill

I took their lives away
Seven dead, lying rotten
Unburied victims
Their naked bodies putrefy

Strangulation caused her death
Just like all the others
Raped before and after death
Stripped, naked, tortured

They're all dead, they're all dead
They're all dead, by strangulation

I come alive in the darkness
Left murdered and nameless
Dead unburied and rotten
Half eaten by insects

They think they know who I am
All they know is I love to kill
Face down, dead on the ground
Find me before another is found

ALEX WEBSTER

I remember we rehearsed this up at the Music Mall in Buffalo, which was our second rehearsal space. 'Stripped' was written there, as was most of The Bleeding. We worked on it together and tried our best to come up with something that was catchy but still heavy.

That's the challenge in death metal: we want everything to have hooks and be memorable without losing any of the brutality. In our older stuff, we tried to have this catchy stuff but some of the songs meander a little, and the structures aren't super-catchy, unlike the riffs themselves. On Butchered At Birth there are some really long songs that lose their way a little. 'Stripped' was one of our best attempts by that point at writing a song that had dynamics, with parts that built up and had climaxes.

We're really proud of this song, and it's in the top five fan favourites, with 'Hammer Smashed Face' being number one, of course.

PAUL MAZURKIEWICZ

Barnes's original lyrics for the "She was so beautiful..." line were "She was so beautiful, she stole part of my soul." We freaked out and said, "What? Are you writing a love song here?" and so he rewrote the line.

DEVOURED BY VERMIN

LYRICS: WEBSTER · MUSIC: WEBSTER, BARRETT

Ravenous waves attack, drawn by the scent of life

Fever for our blood

Instinct rules this mass, ruthless living sea

Devouring

Countless vermin gnashing at my face

Tear meat from my skull

Swarming, rabid, features are erased

Unrecognizable

Body covered, rat-filled innards

Shred internal organs

Heart and lungs consumed from inside but my pain doesn't end

I have not died

Devour, cesspool of vermin

Devour, bloodthirsty rabid

Devoured by vermin

Resistance now gives way, the rodents freely feed

Tearing at my skin

Muscles are exposed, shining red with blood

Meat that they seek

Crawling rodents gorging on me

Repulsive starving droves

Shredding, stripping, consuming all I was

Tissue pulled from bones

Dying slowly, feeling every fang

Shock has yet to come

Scavengers tear out my eyes

My pain won't end, I have not died

Devour, cesspool of vermin

Devour, bloodthirsty rabid

Devoured by vermin

Ruthless gnawing vermin feed

Cleaning off my bones while I breathe

Stenching greasy rodents swarm

My body is losing its form

Devour, cesspool of vermin

Devour, bloodthirsty rabid

Devoured by vermin

ALEX WEBSTER

We dismissed Chris from the band in the middle of recording the Vile album, and that left us having to rewrite everything. This song was already called 'Devoured by Vermin,' and although we scrapped Chris's lyrics and rewrote them, the general idea was the same. It's literally about a person being eaten by rats: the vermin aren't some metaphorical evil enemy of the guy in the song—it's literally rats.

We're usually pretty literal: there aren't any hidden meanings. Coming up with the subject matter wasn't hard: the big challenge for me, which I hadn't foreseen and took us a while to get used to, was fitting the lyrics into the music and making them catchy. During that process, and from there on out, we appreciated more what Chris had done in the band, and how hard his job was. We'd taken that for granted. Once we started having to do that work ourselves, we realised what a good job he'd done and that it wasn't as easy as it looked.

I WILL KILL YOU

LYRICS AND MUSIC: WEBSTER

Bleed for my pain
Revenge on treacherous snakes
They will pay

Slicing the flesh
Sculptured wounds my catharsis
I will stain

Into the heart
Needle injects gasoline
Convulsions

The one that they betrayed
Has made them this way

Plagued by the bastards
I will kill you
Killed by my rage

Scream at my face
The grisly scars went unavenged
Until now

Deep in the hole
You are not gagged and scream aloud
But unheard

Choke on your vomit
You watch your hands cut off
Then your legs

The one that you betrayed
Will kill you this way

Scarred by the bastards

I will kill you
Killed by my rage
I must kill you

Into the throat
The scalpel slices
Warm blood sprays out
The gushing entices

Pull out your heart
And let you watch
Shove in your mouth
Then stab your crotch

I watch your agony

I am released
From years of pain
Your death averted
My becoming insane
You are dead

ALEX WEBSTER

When I write lyrics for a fast, aggressive song like this one, I tend to write lyrics that are just about somebody completely losing their shit and killing someone out of hatred. Look at 'Puncture Wound Massacre' and 'Crushing the Despised', for example. These are not songs about serial killers or anything like that, they're just about someone killing an extremely hated enemy in a fit of rage.

I didn't have anyone in particular as the target of this song, but everyone can relate to being stabbed in the back or people talking shit about you. Obviously, in the real world you don't kill those people, but in the horror fantasy stories that we tell in our songs, the character doesn't have that restraint and he goes out and kills for revenge. Vengeance is definitely a big theme in a lot of the songs I write, but don't worry, I'm not carrying round a bunch of hate or anything like that. It's just something that this music makes me think of.

For the line about injecting gasoline into someone's heart, I was reading a lot of Mafia and crime books at the time, so maybe I got it from those. Or maybe I just thought that would kill you. It seems like it would!

RANDY BLYTHE, LAMB OF GOD

In my expert opinion, there is one song that fully encapsulates the genius that is Cannibal Corpse, and that song is, of course, 'I Will Kill You.' Over extremely punishing riffs and drums—because all death metal riffs and drums should be punishing: if they are not, they are not death metal—and in simple, no-nonsense, layman's terms, they explain exactly what death metal is really all about: hot sex. Cleverly disguised as an act of random violence, 'I Will Kill You' is really an ode to seduction and sweet, mutually-agreed-upon consummation. From flirting, to foreplay, to intercourse, to post-coitus bliss, the chorus of 'I Will Kill You' lays it all out in a tender, logical progression. "I will kill you (Hey good-looking, let's stop screwing around here, leave the bar, and get back to my hotel room for some hanky-panky), I must kill you (Damn, you're driving me crazy with desire! You look so good nekkid!), you are dead (Yeah, you like that don't ya? My God, you're beautiful!, I have killed you (Whew! That was great! Pass me the cigarettes. What's that? You can't move? Yeeeeeeeah, I rocked your world for sure!)." This is some next-level Casanova-type shit. Some may balk at Cannibal Corpse's seemingly "violent" lyrics, but underneath the brutal image, these are sensitive, romantic gentlemen: the Don Juans of death metal. If I were to try and lure a lady to the bedchamber, I would want to come across as confident (ie 'I WILL KILL YOU'), not wimpy. The Corpse is not wimpy. Hails!

ROB BARRETT

CANNIBAL CORPSE'S 'QUIET ONE' DIGS DEEP INTO
HIS MEMORIES OF A LIFE IN METAL.

I was born on January 29, 1970, in Buffalo. I have an older half-brother, Mike, and an older half-sister, Denise. My grandmother played the piano in church, and she left me the electric organ she used to play on when she passed on, which was cool because I used to mess around on it when I was a kid. Organ is similar to the guitar in a strange kind of way.

I was good in school until the teenage years, when some kind of rebellion took over. I had to deal with some undesirables at a vocational school that I chose to go to. I picked the wrong school, basically: it was on the east side of Buffalo, which is a tough place. The school was Seneca Vocational High School and its address was 666 East Delavan Avenue, if you can imagine that... I was interested in electrical stuff and they had a program there, but I should have chosen a school called McKinley, where all my other friends went to. But I learned quick.

Freshman year was pretty rough on me. I was hassled a lot by older kids. Fortunately I had a couple of senior friends who were into metal and would look out for me. Every day we would have to drive by three other high schools, and there was a lot of rivalry going on. I tried to avoid getting into fights, though: I was never one of those brawling kids. I started ditching school a lot, though, because I didn't want to deal with the pressure of kids messing around with me because I was the new kid. I would check in at the home room and then ditch out. They caught onto it after a while and the principal told me I had the worst attendance history in the history of the school. So they kicked me out.

I had a tutor for a little while. He knew that I wasn't just some dumb kid and understood that I just didn't want to deal with the shit, and offered to teach me for free in the local library for a few weeks. Then I was sent to Buffalo Alternative High School, where the bad kids go, which just made things worse. It was like a detention center for troublemakers. On the first day I sat down and some kid said "Hey, that's my seat." I thought "Fuck this" and said "It's my seat now!" and it turned into the usual "I'll see you after school!" stuff. A bunch of my friends came along too, so the fight never happened. They all carried knives, so I ended up carrying a knife too. I ended up skipping out of that school as well. Then I went to a satellite school near my house, but I quit a couple of months before graduation.

All this stuff didn't really bother me. I had my own circle of friends, but I was happy being alone as well. I also had music to rely on. My father listened to music every night when I was a kid. He would listen to everything—Yardbirds, ELO, Deep Purple, Black Sabbath, a wide range of stuff. He even had Iron Maiden and Judas Priest albums. It was good exposure for me. I had all those songs memorized before I even started playing guitar. It was definitely a healthy musical home. Even today my parents love my music: they have Cannibal's albums in show cases.

I got obsessed with MTV when that started. I wanted to know how music was made: I'd be glued to the guitar players and watch how they played. Then a friend of my brother sold me his guitar, a Gibson L6S which I bought for $12. I used to pretend I was playing it. Even when I was a little kid I used to play air guitar on tennis rackets. Then I tried a guitar that belonged to a friend of mine in a band, and played along note for

note with the song they were playing. The guys in the band freaked out and told me I had to get a guitar. Then in 1985 I begged my mom for a guitar—"Please mom, I'll never ask you for anything again!"—and I got a Cort Flying V and a practice amp. I tuned my guitar to whatever albums I wanted to learn and started learning songs.

By 1986 I was skipping school and going to a friend's house to smoke weed and play guitar. One of my friends from the alternative school was Jason Blachowitz, who later played bass in Malevolent Creation. He had a WASP backpatch and I thought "This dude's cool, he likes metal!" I asked him if he wanted to skip school and he said "Yeah! Want to come to my house and jam?" He had a bass and told me he wanted to start a band called Destroyer. I was really into Kiss so that sounded cool. I loved Cheap Trick and AC/DC too. We'd yell along with those songs.

I started trying to get a band together in 1986. The first one was with a couple of guys from the neighborhood, and we called it Dark Deception. It was me, a bass player called Scott O'Dell, a drummer called Bob D'Alimonte, a guitarist called Jim Block and a singer, Mike Paravalos. They all went to McKinley High, where I should have gone to. At first we just played songs by Sabbath, Priest, Maiden, Metallica and Ozzy, and then we started writing our own stuff, which wasn't really that great but it was a start.

I met Alex and Jack in their band Beyond Death in 1987, and Paul and Bob in Tirant Sin. I met all those guys right around the same time. We all used to practice in this building called Absolute Storage. The first show that Dark Deception did was with Tirant Sin and Beyond Death, and I think it was Beyond Death's first show as well. Alex was singing. Afterwards Alex told me they were looking for another guitarist, so I gave him Frank Lombardi's number. It was cool that we all helped each other out that way.

Dark Deception fizzled out around 1988, when Tirant Sin and Beyond Death came together as Cannibal Corpse. I wanted to move out of Buffalo because I thought nothing special was happening, and I was inspired to move to Florida because Cannibal played a show with Cynic and Malevolent down there: Malevolent had already moved down there in 1986 or '87. The drummer for Cynic was amazing, and I thought "If there's musicians like this down there, that's where I want to go."

So I told our drummer Bob D'Alimonte that we should save up and move to Fort Lauderdale, which we did in December 1989. It was me, Jason, Bob and Jeff Juszkiewicz, who was on Malevolent Creation's The Ten Commandments. We were all jamming together and talking about being a band, but it was more or less just jamming. When I got there, my focus was finding serious musicians. I didn't want to waste time, so I hung out with the Cynic guys in Miami and they introduced me to Alex Marquez and Dennis Muñoz and I started Solstice with them.

Things really started to move for me now, because these were serious guys. We recorded a four-song demo with Jim Morris at Morrisound in 1991, which got an immediate response from the labels—Roadrunner, Relapse, Metal Blade, Nuclear Blast, all of those. Steamhammer responded, because they were mainly thrash-based, and they flew somebody out: we played a showcase for him to see the crowd reaction, and they sent out a contract shortly after that. We knew we had to write four more songs because we were scheduled to record in 1992.

Before that could happen, Phil Fasciana from Malevolent Creation called Alex Marquez and asked him to join them. Alex said that I had to come with him as a package deal, so we went to jam with Malevolent and wrote the Retribution album within a month. We recorded that with Scott Burns in January 1992 and then did the Solstice album that same May. We weren't rushing it: we took our time, but that was a crazy juggling of the two bands.

We then toured with Malevolent Creation, Obituary, Agnostic Front and Cannibal Corpse. It was called the Complete Control Tour. We were splitting a bus with Cannibal, which probably led to them calling me in December 1992 when they got rid of Bob Rusay. They knew me from the road and figured it could work out. I was working as a bike courier down in Miami when Alex called me and asked if I could fly up and help them out with some tours. I said "Of course!", because we'd been friends for a while: it was really cool that they considered me.

I went up there and we toured with Epidemic and Unleashed, starting in January 1993. I only had two weeks to learn Cannibal's set, but fortunately I knew the songs because I'd known the band since they first got together. I saw them play with Dark Angel, way back when. I was proud that they were kicking ass, and it made total sense for me to play with them. Their style was abrasive and really mayhemic: back then, it was a "race to the end of the song" attitude and everything was a bit rough around the edges, but that's what gave Cannibal their signature sound. It was raw, at the beginning anyway. I was laughing about it, saying "How do you come up with these riffs? They're really weird!"

SENTENCED TO BURN

LYRICS AND MUSIC: WEBSTER

Follow the one
Evil masked in pride
Charisma to lead
Speeches laced with hate

Leading the dense
The bovine human herd
Inherently stupid
The fools deserve this fate

Warfare begins
Cities are ablaze
Tortured screams
Skin turning black

Carbonization
They will all burn
Mass execution
They will all die

Burning the world
And all of its life
Throwing all the people
In a pit of fire

Watching the sheep
Gathering to die
Followers in life
Follow to the grave

Follow the one
Evil masked in pride
Charisma to lead
Speeches laced with hate

Leading the dense
The bovine human herd
Inherently stupid
The fools deserve this fate

Warfare begins
Cities are ablaze
Tortured screams
Skin turning black

Carbonization
They will all burn
Mass execution
They will all die

Pile the bodies
Set them aflame
The human race
Sentenced to burn

Burning flesh
Miasma of their death
Civilisation
It is destroyed

Pits of corpses
Unholy grave of war
Hanging victims
Guilty of free thought

Warfare begins
Cities are ablaze
Tortured screams
Skin turning black

Carbonization
They will all burn
Mass execution
They will all die

Pile the bodies
Set them aflame
The human race
Sentenced to burn
Pile the bodies
Set them aflame
The human race
Sentenced to burn

War of fire shred their souls
Burn in hell doomsday's toll
Failed to see the trap they laid
Demagogues lead them into
the flames

Pile the bodies
Set them aflame
The human race
Sentenced to burn
Pile the bodies
Set them aflame
The human race
Sentenced to burn

ALEX WEBSTER

This is about any demagogue, and it's pretty much the only song where I try to dip into a slightly deeper meaning. It still has plenty of horror, with piles of bodies and so on, but it's definitely the only song of mine that is a little bit political. I can't stand people who appeal to a mob mentality, but it happens everywhere. It's human nature, I guess, to follow those kinds of people, but our species would do well to get past listening to that kind of talk and following it. Without leaders convincing groups of people to kill each other, there wouldn't be war. National pride is one of the motivators, which is more or less what I'm talking about here.

STABBED IN THE THROAT

LYRICS: MAZURKIEWICZ · MUSIC: O'BRIEN

As the blood begins to gush out the side of your neck
I thrust my cold steel into your face, you're closer to death
A twelve-inch blade will help decide your ultimate fate
This summons to die has been given to you for accepting my hate

Stabbed in the throat
For no reason but to kill, for no reason but the thrill
You must die for me to survive
Stabbed in the throat
I believe in sacrifice, sliced open with my knife
Your body is now life deprived

Vocal cords twitching, esophagus severed, a hemorrhaging brain
Your lacerated jugular vein is spurting away
As mortality fades I am ready to flay your whole body and head
Vigorously carving this fresh human flesh, I am one with the dead

Stabbed in the throat
For no reason but to kill, for no reason but the thrill
You must die for me to survive
Stabbed in the throat
I believe in sacrifice, sliced open with my knife
Your body is now life deprived

I'm chewing bloody skin from the cadaver
Consuming lifeless meat, mangled and tattered
Half-eaten corpse lies skinless in the gutter
I am revitalized

Odium, embedded in my skull

To kill and eat your prey a way of nature
The taste of death must consciously be savored
My cannibal existence never dangered
Just look into my eyes

Subjugate, intensity to blame

Gnawing on the head, sliced to fucking shreds
Knife to the gullet results in cessation

Stabbed in the throat
For no reason but to kill, for no reason but the thrill
You must die for me to survive
Stabbed in the throat
I Believe in sacrifice, sliced open with my knife
Your body is now life deprived

PAUL MAZURKIEWICZ:
This song is pretty blunt—it's about a maniac who wants to kill someone. I used the word "odium" in it, which is cool. What does it mean? No idea. I wouldn't write that way these days: I use words that everybody uses.

Every song that Pat has written for Cannibal Corpse, I've written the lyrics for, except for 'Infinite Misery' of course, because it's an instrumental. We work well together. Pat's songwriting can be really technical, which has made it difficult to write lyrics for in the past, but we've got used to each other's style by now and it's become easier, I know how he writes now. 'Stabbed in the Throat' was the first song that Pat wrote for Cannibal. I was still a little fresh when it came to writing lyrics, but I think it came out pretty well.

It's a case of finding lines which work best in certain parts, so if there's a part which has a ton of notes I might let it breathe, so that people can hear how crazy it is with no lyrics there. In this song I used a dictionary and a thesaurus to come up with the necessary vocabulary, and played off certain words. 'Kill' is a word we use a lot in our songs, so it's useful to have a thesaurus because it tells you how many synonyms there for it. I think we've used most of them over the years...

POUNDED INTO DUST

LYRICS AND MUSIC: WEBSTER

Forces of hate meet
Gather for the siege
Encircling their foe
The raid begins
Their revenge is sought
Through violence, smashing, killing, stabbing, pounding
Iron weapons clash
Evil warriors strike
Hammers cracking skulls
Axes chopping heads
Their revenge is now
Through violence, crushing, maiming, hacking, pounding

Blood soaks the ground
In their own, they will drown
Surrounded by disgust
Pounded into dust

Battle rages on
Bleeding wounded scream
Clubs shatter bones
Swords sever limbs
Their blind rage compels
Their frenzy, bloodlust, madness, burning, hatred
Berzerkers overwhelm
Defenders run in fear
No prisoners today
The end is near
Their blind rage endless

No mercy lay waste; wipe out, kill them, kill them

Their struggle to defend
The attack will never end
Surrounded by disgust
Pounded into dust

The captured will be crucified as a warning to the rest
When the killing is completed the city will be burned
Their way of life will be destroyed, no trace of them remains

Annihilate
They lay waste
Eradicate
Victory for their hatred, fury, raging, pounding

Blood soaks the ground
In their own, they will drown
Surrounded by disgust
Pounded into dust

ALEX WEBSTER

It was challenging to write these lyrics and squeeze them into the song, and also for George to sing them, although he did a truly amazing job of making them a reality. I like the whole idea of ancient battles, where there were no firearms involved and people pounded on each other with clubs or speared each other, like Braveheart or any epic film. I covered the same thing on 'The Time to Kill is Now.'

This was another song that I thought would be good to be totally fast from start to finish – a relentless assault with lyrics about an enemy being destroyed. It has that stabbing, pounding, punching part to it right before the chorus, like 'Hammer Smashed Face' does. I love those parts: they don't have to be complicated. If they were, they'd detract from that primitive intensity that we want.

DEAD HUMAN COLLECTION

LYRICS: MAZURKIEWICZ · MUSIC: O'BRIEN

I cannot scream, my mouth is wired shut

I cannot see, my eyes are filled with blood

I must die while suffering

Pawn of torturous punishment

Losing all reason to live

Cherishing this painful death

To become part of the...

Dead human collection

Dead human collection

I cannot hear with punctured ear drums

I can barely breathe

My ribs are crushed

I will die while suffering

Maimed, repulsive menagerie

Collection for the insane

Closer to death I become

I want to be one with the dead

Collection of dead humans, dead

I want to be one with the dead

Collection of dead humans, dead

I want to be one of them

Compilation obscene

An assembly for psychotic malefaction

Virulent anarchy

The final member of this vile congregation

I cannot scream, my mouth is wired shut

I cannot see, my eyes turned into dust

I died into the...

Dead human collection

Dead human

Dead human

Dead human collection

PAUL MAZURKIEWICZ

In 90 percent of the songs we write, we have the title before we do any actual writing of music or lyrics. So with 'Dead Human Collection,' I asked myself what it would feel like to be part of a collection—tied up and and unable to breathe. It's horrible. The guy in the story is supposed to the collector, who joins his collection of dead bodies when he dies himself. He ultimately becomes one with the dead, to complete the collection.

DROWNING IN VISCERA

LYRICS: MAZURKEWICZ · MUSIC: O'BRIEN

Engulfed in the innards
Of rotting cadavers a rancid gore sea
Asphyxiation
Tangled intestines become my reality
Choking on guts
Asphyxiation gasping for breath
Drowning in viscera

Slowly to taper away dissipate
Absorbing this ultimate carnage
Surrounding me
Soaking in entrails decayed
Decomposed

Entombed without reason
In moist isolation of repugnancy
Morose sensation
Covered completely as terror
Enhances pain, to suffocate
Morose sensation gasping for breath
Drowning in viscera

Sinking in this tamped hell, pestilent
Smothered in heaping chunks
Stinking flesh putrefies
Decomposition ensures burial
Inundated languid doom

Iniquity, submerged ending
Primeval swamp, sanguinary

Inescapable abuse

Starting to fade, blood saturates
Deadly embrace, immolated
Imbued with pus of the dead

Eviscerate another life gutted soul
Morbidity, obliterate
Engrossing plight fatal rot
Consuming scum
Drenched in evil excrement
Sent to a world to die in pain by
Drowning in viscera

Engulfed in the innards
Of rotting cadavers a rancid gore sea
Asphyxiation
Tangled intestines become my reality
Choking on guts
Morose sensation gasping for breath
Drowning in viscera

Eviscerate another life gutted soul
Morbidity, obliterate
Engrossing plight fatal rot
Consuming scum
Drenched in evil excrement
Sent to a world to die in pain by
Drowning in viscera

PAUL MAZURKIEWICZ

This is typical Cannibal gore: the title says it all. There's no twist to the story or anything: it's literally about drowning in viscera and being engulfed in innards. It's like a nightmare in words. I haven't thought about this song in a long time, actually. It's about being helpless in a terrible situation. Not fun.

SANDED FACELESS

LYRICS: MAZURKEWICZ · MUSIC: O'BRIEN

Rapacious for pleasure scraping
Filing down with intense grinding
Harsh abrasive friction deface
Countenance now removed forever

Scouring faces with flies
Tedious rasping
Painstakingly grate the skin
Insensate razing
Sanded faceless
A violent facial scrub
Malefic in nature
An art of shaving the bone
Insalubrious
Sanded faceless

Rubbing off a human's visage
Enduring display of malice
With celerity they perish
Countenance now removed forever

Everything gone from the head
Miasmal menace
All curves of a face are now smooth
Forced a new surface

Sanded faceless
Obscurity into black
Outrageous agenda
Sensory perception lost
Left to die in pain
Sanded faceless

Insane appearance eyeless
To calibrate the skull
Image erasing soulless
Retexturing of flesh
Suddenly to be faceless
For perpetuity

Scouring faces with flies
Tedious rasping
Painstakingly grate the skin
Insensate razing
Sanded faceless
A violent facial scrub
Malefic in nature
An art of shaving the bone
Insalubrious
Sanded faceless

PAUL MAZURKIEWICZ

This was Pat's idea. It's pretty brutal. We're always trying to think outside the box when it comes to writing about doing damage to people.

PAT O'BRIEN

I came up with the concept of taking an electric sander and sanding someone's face off with it. It came from the painting job which I had for the longest time. I was pissed off with someone I knew, and I was sanding a door at my house and picturing his face under the sander.

I was born in Batavia, New York, on October 25, 1969. I thought for the longest time that I was born in Buffalo, New York, but I was wrong. Batavia is a small city between Buffalo and Rochester. It's about the halfway point between those two cities and it's really close to the small town of Akron where I grew up. I have two brothers, one 10 years younger and the other three years older.

My childhood was pretty happy. My parents were together the whole time. I was never a particularly athletic kid or anything like that, although I played soccer for a little while at a very amateur level until I was about 12. My upbringing was very like the Andy Griffith Show in that Akron is a very small American town with two policemen and no traffic lights—a very country place. The Fourth of July parade and the carnival are a big deal each year. Everybody knows everybody else, and we can leave our car doors unlocked there. It wasn't a rich place: just a modest village.

For miles around Akron, there was just country. It's very much a part of the Great Lakes region: our accent is Great Lakes, as is our vocabulary. Culturally, the nearest big city,

Buffalo, is probably more like Detroit or Cleveland than New York City. It's a steel town with mills and factories, although a lot of those had closed by the time that I was a teenager.

Our house, and my grandparents' house, were both over 100 years old, which is unusual in the States because a lot of people have new houses. There were gravestones so old in the local cemetery that they had German inscriptions on them, because the area was mainly settled by German and English people. My dad's side of the family was Methodist, and my mom's side was Mennonite. My father wasn't particularly religious but my mother was, and when I was young I often attended church and Sunday School.

Throughout my youth, we lived on Cedar Street in Akron, and right behind it was a little house where my mother's parents lived. My father's parents lived nearby on John Street, so all of my grandparents lived less than a two-minute walk away from my house. It was definitely beneficial for me: my family was in my life a lot.

I'm mentioning this because readers of this book will probably find it strange, given the kind of band I'm in, but I really had one of the most wholesome, all-American upbringings a kid could hope for. I can't even believe it was like that, having lived in cities for a few years now. Nowadays, I could be in a cabin in the middle of Alaska and I would still lock the doors.

In Akron Central School, kindergarten through grade 12 was in the same building. One half of the building was dedicated to K through six, and the other half was for seven through 12. I went through the whole thing. I walked there every day.

There was a train track where we played all the time. We loved it there. My parents and my father's parents owned 40 acres of woods near there and I would go back there and run around. We'd go hunting and stuff like that. My grandfather was in the NRA and was really into the old muzzle-loading guns. He had a bearskin rug from a bear that he'd killed. He was just about the only person in New York State that I met with a pistol permit, apart from policemen. Permits were hard to come by and required a lot of rigorous background checks.

I loved shooting for a couple of years, and we'd hunt rabbits and squirrels. Everybody hunted, it was normal. This will make people in Europe laugh when they read this, I realize, but I did most of my shooting before the age of 18. We were very safe about it: I took a hunting safety course and had a license. I spent whatever money I had on .22 rounds, and we'd shoot bottles and stuff, and then I had a shotgun when I was 16. After that I got into bass and kind of lost interest in guns and hunting.

Around the time I was born, my dad worked at Calspan, which was a technology company. After that he worked as the head librarian at the University of Buffalo in the Science and Engineering Library. He actually wrote a couple of books about how to find reference materials: they're not gripping page-turners by any means, but they were necessary tools for students.

At first, I did really well at school. I became an underachiever at high school, at the age of 15 or 16, because I lost interest in everything except having fun and playing music. I still did pretty well but I could have done better if I'd really applied myself. I went to college for five semesters, or basically two and a half years, and then I took a sixth semester off in the fall of 1991 because Cannibal had a tour coming up. I had declared history, because I couldn't think of anything else and I liked it.

As long as I can remember, I have loved music. As soon as I could hear it, I loved it. Both my parents were very into music. My dad loved traditional Scottish music and learned to play the bagpipes. He ended up playing it really well: he was in a band called the Gordon Highlanders in Buffalo. They went around and did parades on the Fourth of July in Western New York and southern Ontario. My dad would march around in circles in the backyard, practicing the bagpipes. I remember he had a friend who would give him a hard time about it and say, "My God, stop playing that awful noise!" The whole neighborhood knew that my dad was the guy with the bagpipes. I loved the drone and the melody over the top of it. So I grew up with bagpipe music.

Beyond that, my parents listened to a ton of country music. I never cared for it that much but I did like some of the bluegrass stuff, with the fast picking. I did like the old rock'n'roll records that my dad had from his teenage years in the Fifties, though. He had a bunch of 45s by Elvis, Chuck Berry and Fats Domino which I listened to and loved. I would also listen to classical music. Our local library had three or four cassette decks, headphones and a bunch of cassettes, which was a big deal in the late Seventies. Apart from a Wings cassette, most of them were classical music. I'd go to the library and listen to Tchaikovsky's '1812 Overture,' which I loved because it had cannons in it. It was very powerful. I still go back and listen to those pieces once in a while.

I wanted to play guitar when I was six, which would have been 1976. I took some lessons, but the only place I could find that taught the guitar had really boring folk songs, very simple stuff which didn't grab me, so after three or four months I quit. I also tried making a drum when I was real little, because I wanted to play drums in my dad's pipe band when I grew up. He'd march around the back yard playing bagpipes, so I made a little drum out of a butter tub

and attached it to my belt. I played it with little sticks and followed my dad around. So I've always wanted to play something.

Music has always been in my family: my mom had taught herself to play the piano relatively well. When I was losing interest in the guitar, they wanted to keep me with it so she took up the guitar as well. Even after I told her that I just wanted to play, rather than learn 'Michael Row the Boat Ashore' or those other songs, she liked the guitar so much that she stuck with it for a while. Both of my brothers played trumpet in the school band.

Later, I started getting into whatever was on the radio: regular stuff like Huey Lewis & the News. I also liked new wave acts like Devo and Blondie in the late 70s and early 80s. I still love Devo to this day. Then I joined the Boy Scouts and that was a big thing, because we'd go camping and some of the guys would be listening to Molly Hatchet and AC/DC. I started to like that stuff, and then a friend of mine asked me "Have you heard this band Mötley Crüe?" and played me their first or second album in about 1982. He had another friend with a suitcase full of cassettes of cool stuff, and we used to go over to his house and listen to all this heavy music—Accept among them, who I got into in a really big way, plus Iron Maiden of course, and Rush. I learned a lot from the older kids. That was pretty much when the floodgates opened for me, around the age of 12 or 13. There was no turning back: I just loved metal.

Right about then I realised that I had to revisit the idea of playing an instrument, and I started playing bass when I was around 14, in 1984. I'd had about a year of listening to metal and I was like "I can't take it. I gotta play something!" All my friends wanted to play some instrument. We all loved that kind of music and I remember listening to some of these bands and thinking that I loved how the bass sounded. It sounded cool underneath the music. I'd listen to Peter Baltes from Accept or Cliff Williams from AC/DC and I liked the way the bass was the foundation under the guitar riffs.

Later, when I got into thrash metal, the bass tended to mesh with the drums into one big rhythm section, but back when I was listening to standard heavy rock and metal, the drums and the bass were really together. I also thought to myself that I could never play what Angus Young or Eddie Van Halen did, but that I was pretty sure I could do what Cliff Williams and Michael Anthony did. With all due respect to them, they weren't playing with the chops that the lead guitarists had, and so I went to the one music store in the town next to Akron and rented a really bad Fender Jazz bass copy that was probably worth about $100 when it was brand new.

A kid who was three years older than me gave me some lessons, a friend from Scouts named Mike Hudson, who was the bass player in the school jazz band. He also played tuba, because you had to play a brass instrument in that band. They were going to try and get me into the jazz band, and I was up for giving it a go, but they told me I would have to learn the

trombone, which I didn't want to do. Mike did a good job, teaching me out of the first Mel Bay book. I paid him five bucks a lesson. It took a while to get any good, though, because the most important thing for me was getting into a band and playing with other people. That was what I wanted to do more than anything.

I had a friend who played drums named Don Roth and another called Dan Hudson, who was Mike's little brother, who played guitar. With another guitarist, Tony Fritz, we all got together in 1984 and played the Scorpions' 'Rock You like a Hurricane' 15 times! We thought it was so awesome. There's nothing like playing in a band. It was so cool to hear how your instrument worked with the other instruments, and I loved it.

Thrash metal came after I started listening to any radio show I could find: there was one in Buffalo and another in Toronto. The Toronto one had a show called Q107's Midnight Metal

Hour and they would play Razor, Voivod and Celtic Frost. I heard 'Beyond the North Winds' from To Mega Therion in 1985 or '86: that song is so heavy.

Metal radio shows from Canada had an influence on us down in Western New York, since we could pick up the signal due to our proximity to Toronto. I heard 'Seek and Destroy' and 'For

Whom the Bell Tolls' by Metallica on Q107's Midnight Metal Hour: they were heavy and I liked them. Later, I went to scout camp and this one dude had heard me playing Accept on my little radio in my tent. He said "You like metal, man? Check this shit out!" and played me 'Fight Fire with Fire' from Metallica's Ride the Lightning. I just could not understand the double picking and thrash beats: I was like "How are they doing this? How are they making these sounds?" I'd never heard palm-muting like that, and precise, up- and down-picking. Normally when you play like that you can hear the upstroke and the downstroke, but James Hetfield's picking on 'Fight Fire with Fire' is so perfectly muted that it almost sounded like all downstrokes, but at a literally impossible speed. It blew my mind. I was like, "This is the best shit I've ever heard in my fuckin' life!" That song had a massive impact on me: I had to buy it as soon as I got home from camp. That was in the summer of 1985.

I'm not sure if I picked up on what Cliff Burton was doing with the bass guitar. Right after that I got Kill 'Em All and if they hadn't told me that '(Anesthesia) Pulling Teeth' was a bass guitar, I wouldn't have been able to tell, because of the guitar-like tone he was able to get with distortion and a wah pedal and harmonics. He totally impressed me, though. His playing was killer.

I heard Slayer shortly after that. I think Hell Awaits was the first album I heard of theirs. Living out in the country, I was a little bit behind some of my friends in the city, who had other friends with more access to music. I didn't get to go to any cool record stores in Buffalo or New York, because it was just too far, at least when I was too young to drive. You're not going to make your parents drive 20 miles to buy some album.

Sodom were a death metal band to me. I bought Obsessed by Cruelty in 1986 and I remember taking it home and playing it: it was a real revelation. Even though it was sloppy compared to the other stuff that I'd heard, it sounded really evil. The tempo was quite a bit faster than anything I'd heard up to that point, and I was blown away. I loved that dark, scary atmosphere, because I also loved horror movies.

In the 70s, you'd get films on TV about hauntings and the supernatural, although they were heavily cut, of course: those were the things that I found frightening. The Exorcist, Burnt Offerings, The Sentinel: those were really good movies that scared me when I was a kid. Coming from a religious background, I thought this stuff was real. It gets very cold where we lived, and there would be a lot of very cold, spooky nights outside when it would be five degrees outside and blowing a fierce gale. All the leaves would be dead, and in the fall and wintertime our house really lent itself to feeling haunted. It's a vibe you get up in the north. You get it in England too, where there's a bunch of creepy old houses.

So I would watch, say, Burnt Offerings, and I was genuinely scared. At the age of nine or 10 I saw The Exorcist and I thought that Satan was coming for me—it freaked me the fuck out. So did Phantasm. Holy crap, that was scary! And totally warped too. The Shining was sick as well. It's one of the things I miss about not being religious. I gradually grew out of my religious belief until finally there was a point where supernatural stories failed to inspire genuine fear for me any more.

So we were just jamming and having fun, getting together at each other's houses and playing with whoever came along. I loved jamming. We would cover regular rock songs as well as metal tunes. I did one cover-band show at school with some friends: we played Bruce Springsteen and Bob Seger songs: 'Turn the Page' was one of them. That would have been in about 1986: I already loved thrash metal by then, but I just wanted to play, and that was the only opportunity I had out there. That one show was my first time on stage. We were beginner musicians and we were having fun. That band lasted about a month.

After that I started playing with Jack Owen and Darrin Pfeiffer, who became the core of Beyond Death. I'd known Jack since third grade, and Darrin since first grade. We all grew up together. We got together in late 1986 and immediately began trying to play Metallica's 'Seek and Destroy' and Slayer's 'Die by the Sword'. I was singing on the Slayer song, but I don't remember who sang on 'Seek and Destroy': maybe it was Darrin. That was my senior year in high school and I was doing a course in music theory.

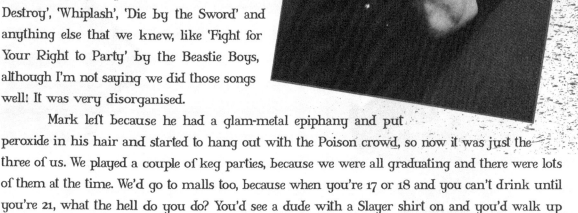

One of the field trips for that course was a classical guitar seminar, where we got to go see a guitar quartet. I was blown away by that. There were two long-haired dudes there from Clarence, the next town over from Akron, and I went over and talked to them and one of them was a guitarist called Mark Caruana. He said he was into Metallica so we traded numbers. So now it was Jack, Mark, Darrin and me and we started playing at parties. We did 'Seek and Destroy', 'Whiplash', 'Die by the Sword' and anything else that we knew, like 'Fight for Your Right to Party' by the Beastie Boys, although I'm not saying we did those songs well! It was very disorganised.

Mark left because he had a glam-metal epiphany and put peroxide in his hair and started to hang out with the Poison crowd, so now it was just the three of us. We played a couple of keg parties, because we were all graduating and there were lots of them at the time. We'd go to malls too, because when you're 17 or 18 and you can't drink until you're 21, what the hell do you do? You'd see a dude with a Slayer shirt on and you'd walk up and ask him where the party is. He might be from a different neighborhood, so you'd end up meeting different girls than the same handful you've been hitting on from your own.

Me, Jack and Darrin were the Akron kids, meeting metalheads from these various communities around Buffalo, and one particular band name kept coming up: Humongous. They were a traditional heavy metal band, one of the biggest in Buffalo. The biggest was Talas, Billy Sheehan's band, but they were really hard rock rather than metal. Zillion was another big band from there. Anyway, we kept hearing about this band Humongous when we were hanging out in music stores. This was the 80s, so obviously there was no internet, and to meet people you actually went and met them. We had no qualms whatsoever about walking straight up to anyone who had Slayer or Metallica on their shirt or jacket and saying, "Hey, what's going on?"

We made a lot of friends that way, who all told us about Humongous and this place called the Metal Shop up in North Tonawanda, a bit north of Buffalo. We saw that there was a show there with Tirant Sin, Wild Child and Humongous, and we saw them play. Wild Child were a little more hard rock: their bass player, Mario, did all the Billy Sheehan-style tapping stuff and I'm still friends with him to this day.

When we saw Tirant Sin, though, we were like "This is the shit. Holy fuck!" We had no idea that anyone was playing music like that in Western New York, apart from us. Tirant Sin sounded like Slayer and Sodom and Kreator, all rolled into one. We were like, "These guys are fucking amazing!" They were maybe a year older than us and their band was better known. I remember the bass player had a black eye: I found out later that he'd been jumped by 10 jocks on a beach. They looked tough as shit, and we were like "We gotta meet these dudes!"

After the show I exchanged numbers with their guitarist, Bob Rusay. I told him that we had a band called Beyond Death and that we had to do a show together, so we kept in touch. We started going to their shows, and eventually—I think in late 1987—we did a show. It was us and Tirant Sin, who didn't have Chris Barnes yet: he was still in a band called Leviathan at the time, who had done a demo which had gained a lot of popularity on the underground scene, but weren't doing many shows.

Dark Deception opened the show, which was Rob Barrett's band at the time. They were like a Testament-style thrash band. After them was Riff Raff, who were a kind of Van Halen band, and then Tirant Sin headlined. I remember thinking that we sucked compared to Dark Deception. We only practiced once or twice a week, just having fun being noisy and making proto-death metal, but Dark Deception were really skilled: they played an Anthrax song and it sounded exactly like Anthrax. It sounded great.

We knew after that show that we had to step it up and get another guitar player, because we hadn't replaced Mark Caruana when he left. So I called Rob Barrett and asked if he knew anybody who could do it, and he told me about a guy named Frank Lombardi, who became our second guitarist. This dude was great. He came in and played "The Exorcist" by Possessed, and we were like, "Fuck! You're jamming with us if you want to." He had this really good rehearsal room in a storage space, and until then we'd been jamming in Darrin's basement, so we moved into Frank's rehearsal room and started practicing five days a week.

Pretty soon we were playing shows every month, sometimes with Tirant Sin: we became very close with those guys, but towards the end of 1988 it pretty much all ground to a halt. Darrin and Frank were more into DRI and the punk-metal side of things, while me and Jack were discovering new metal bands all the time because we did most of the mail for Beyond Death and sent out most of the demos, so we discovered Morbid Angel and Sadus, and became very influenced by those demos and wanted to make a death metal band.

Then Tirant Sin started having line-up problems: their bass player and guitarist split, so they were left with Chris Barnes, who had joined when Leviathan broke up, Paul Mazurkiewicz and Bob Rusay. Me and Jack were just about done with Beyond Death, because we wanted to do a full-on death metal band, so around late November or early December 1988, I called Bob, and I was like, "Hey man, you guys are looking for a bass player and a guitar player?" He was like "Fuck yeah, man, let's do this!" and we got together. That was it: December 1988, when Cannibal Corpse was formed.

I came up with the name, I'm proud to say: when you've just turned 19 and you're jamming with your friends, you don't expect to think of a name that has staying power like this one. I wanted something death metal,

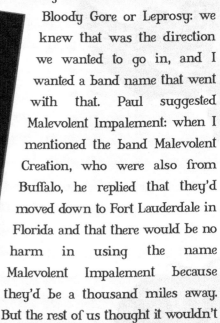

along the lines of Death's Scream Bloody Gore or Leprosy: we knew that was the direction we wanted to go in, and I wanted a band name that went with that. Paul suggested Malevolent Impalement: when I mentioned the band Malevolent Creation, who were also from Buffalo, he replied that they'd moved down to Fort Lauderdale in Florida and that there would be no harm in using the name Malevolent Impalement because they'd be a thousand miles away. But the rest of us thought it wouldn't work. I suggested Cannibal Corpse and after the rest of them thought about it, we agreed that it would be our name. The bands we liked wrote songs about the living dead, and we loved watching films like Day of the Dead and Zombie and The Evil Dead, so to have a band name based on that same theme seemed natural to us.

I'd been working as a packer in a wax products factory, a shitty-ass job that I just did to make money. I wanted to take some time off after graduating high school to put the band together, but my parents weren't happy that I wasn't going to college. At the same time, I continued to work on music with the new band. Bob and Paul already had the music for the song 'A Skull Full of Maggots' when we met them (the title and lyrics came later), and after that we put more songs together. One of the first riffs I wrote was the beginning of 'Put Them to Death'. We had five songs ready for recording within two months, plus two more that were pretty

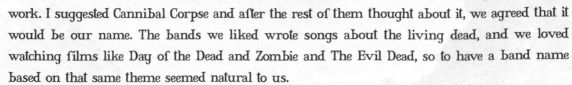

crappy that we didn't end up keeping. When you've got five dudes all writing music together five days a week, you work pretty fast, so we recorded a demo and got ready to play our first show.

We were friends with a promoter named Artie Kwitchoff, him and a guy named Brian Foyster, and they booked us to open for Dark Angel along with two other Buffalo bands, Attakk and Baphomet. Metallica was on tour with Queensryche on the ...And Justice for All album, and they played a week before the Dark Angel show, so Artie—being the smart guy that he is—printed up 5000 flyers and distributed them among the three opening bands, all of whom were going to see Metallica. We handed out flyers all over that fucking show! There were so many that my college roommate Mark 'Psycho' Abramson wound up going backstage to do the college radio show and got Kirk Hammett to sign one of the backs of the flyers. Kirk saw the name and said "Cannibal Corpse? Interesting name!" The flyers were everywhere.

Before that point, local Buffalo shows would get anything between 50 to 100 people: if 100 people came, that was thought to be a massive success, because not many tours came through Buffalo. Bands usually went to Rochester instead. So here we are with Dark Angel at the River Rock Café, with three Buffalo bands opening, and it's our debut show—and 450 people show up! It was well beyond capacity, you could barely move. The crowd went apeshit for us: we sold tons of demos. All the bands had a great night: Dark Angel killed it.

So that was the beginning. More bands came to Buffalo after that show, because their agents must have realised that the city was for real. There was a record store called Home Of The Hits that let us sell our demo and put posters up for our shows. We were on Psycho's radio show every other week. There was a great synergy between the band, the local promoters, the record store and the radio show, as well as the two clubs, the Sky Room and the River Rock Café.

In our first year we opened for Kreator and Coroner, the Accüsed and Blood Feast. We did two shows in 1989 with the Goo Goo Dolls, who were kind of a Hüsker Dü-style band at the time and not too much of a mismatch. We had a really great first year—and we got signed by Metal Blade almost right away.

That is the biggest, most crazy thing of all about the Cannibal Corpse story: we had done a demo in Beyond Death, and Tirant Sin had done three demos, and we had plenty of experience of live shows, but the turnaround between forming Cannibal in December 1988 and being signed in June 1989 was unbelievably quick.

Talking about this now really brings me back to such an exciting time, when everything was happening for us. In 1989, I was in college, in a signed band and playing all over town, as opposed to the previous year, when I was in a significantly smaller band and doing a dead-end job... it's hard to believe!

SEVERED HEAD STONING

LYRICS: WEBSTER · MUSIC: O'BRIEN, WEBSTER

Buried waist-deep, gagged and bound
Piles of heads lie on the ground
Executioners start to assemble

Condemned man shakes with fear
Doom now becoming clear
The faces of the heads he resembles

Severed
Head
Stoning

His family's heads strike him
The most recent victims
Without mercy savage killers throw

His wife's head breaks his jaw
Bruised flesh becoming raw
From many wounds blood begins to flow

When the victim dies
They chop off his head

Severed head stoning

Badly beaten, in a daze
Eye pops out, fluids spray
Pulsing veins cause the wounds to gush

The end is near, the bloody stumps
Mangled face, a mass of lumps
What was now a man reduced to mush

Mashed into a pulp
Dozens of bones break

Severed head stoning

ALEX WEBSTER

I look at this song's lyrics, and I know that it would be a really horrifying thing if it ever happened. It's difficult not to read some Black humour into it, however, because it's so extreme. The people in this song are going to stone someone to death, not with stones but with the severed heads of other victims, which they're throwing at the current victim. It's a pretty outrageous idea, and it would be horrifying if you actually saw it happening. Heads are really heavy, too: it would be exhausting to throw them. Then again, it probably wouldn't take many to hit you to knock you unconscious. I didn't really think through the logistics of making this a reality, but it was a unique, crazy idea for a song.

DECENCY DEFIED

LYRICS AND MUSIC: OWEN

Torn from your body, removed while you scream

Dissect to collect, my blade now reams

Pieces of flesh lie by the side

Worn on my body or put on display

You mark your skin it gives you pleasure

I take your precious art, it becomes my leather

Taking your hide before you have died

Decency defied

Crudely I cut away

All are my prey

Tell me how it feels when your flesh is peeled

You are vain with your art

I desire it torn apart

With my insane hunting, the removal of flesh now starts

You mark your skin, it gives you pleasure

I take your precious art, it becomes my leather

Taking your hide before you have died

Decency defied

To you a design

Now a trophy made mine

To you a design

Now a trophy made mine

I seek to find

To satisfy my fucked mind

I seek to find

To satisfy my fucked mind

Ignoring your cries

Exposing your insides

Violence defined

Torn from your body, removed while you scream

Dissect to collect, my blade now reams

Pieces of flesh lie side by side

Worn on my body or put on display

You mark your skin, it gives you pleasure

I take your precious art, it becomes my leather

Taking your hide before you have died

Decency defied

FRANTIC DISEMBOWELMENT

LYRICS: MAZURKIEWICZ · MUSIC: O'BRIEN

Intestines exposed
By violent thrusts
The innards removes
Dissecting the guts
To rip through the skin
Tissue and muscle
Cartilage shredding
Draining blood vessels

Frenzied hacking
Morals lacking
Eviscerate
Life is gone before my eyes

Flesh matters the most
When splattered around
It's never morose
Absurdly profound
Fresh insides come out
Excitedly done
My purpose in life
To kill just for fun

Frenzied hacking
Morals lacking
Eviscerate
Life is gone before my eyes

Frantic disembowelment
Deprived of vital content
Organ loss without consent
Spastic slicing an event
Sharpened steel my covenant
Frantic disembowelment
Mutilating miscreant
Sickening accomplishment
Spreading gore is time worth spent
Perpetuate this mad intent
Eternally malevolent
Frantic disembowelment

Kidneys exposed
The pancreas flew
Stomach deleted
The spleen I did chew
The carving is over
You lost and I won
Fulfilling my dream
I killed you for fun

Frenzied hacking
Morals lacking
Eviscerate
Life is gone before my eyes

Frantic disembowelment

PAUL MAZURKIEWICZ

This song was definitely a challenge: it's probably Pat's craziest song to date. But it's also one of his most catchy songs, which is why it works as a musical piece without vocals. You could probably listen to 90 percent of our recent stuff without vocals, actually, for that reason. The song patterns flowed with the drum beat and it really worked with the way I accented the stabs of the lyrics.

I'm writing here that "morals are lacking", because the killer know he's wrong to do what's he's doing. That makes it worse than if he was just doing it mindlessly. I was really pleased with the middle section, where the lines all end in "...ent." That's an example of me trying to use sharp sounds to emphasise the point of the song.

PAT Filming 'Frantic Disembowelment' was born out of Alex's frustration that my riffs were going over people's heads. He said, "People need to see this stuff." He was right. So we filmed it and it became a Youtube hit, which was cool.

BLUNT FORCE CASTRATION

LYRICS: MAZURKIEWICZ · MUSIC: O'BRIEN

Smash his scrotum sack
Altered ferociously
Survived this attack
Sterile now left to bleed
Emptied in the crotch
Gonads reduced to pulp
Hateful remedy
Void of sexuality

Sledgehammer destroys
Groin tattered and maimed

Emasculate
Crushing the testicles fast
Debilitate
Cutting off the penis last

Macerate
Deforming
Enervate
Caponized

Detached genitals
Mangled between the thighs
Gelded painfully
Transformed before his eyes
Blood spews everywhere
Deprived of virility

Sledgehammer destroys
Groin tattered and maimed

Inactive
She crushed the testicles fast
Disintegrate
She cut off the penis fast
She cut off the penis last

Inactivate
She crushed the testicles fast
Disintegrate
She cut off the penis last

Macerate
Deforming
Enervate
Caponized

Blunt force castration
Giving life is done
Blunt for castration
Desexualized
Blunt force castration

Macerate
Deforming
Enervate
Caponized

Smash his scrotum sack
Altered ferociously
Survived this attack
Sterile now left to bleed
Hateful remedy
Void of sexuality

Sledgehammer destroys
Castrated with blunt force

PAUL MAZURKIEWICZ

This is an unusual viewpoint for us: a woman torturing a man. We also did that on "Orgasm Through Torture," where the victim is a male and the aggressor is a female. We thought it was a super brutal title: no guy wants to have this happen to him. There are some words here that I would never use nowadays. "Caponized" means having the end of your dick cut off, by the way.

THE TIME TO KILL IS NOW

LYRICS AND MUSIC: WEBSTER

We see them coming a mile away

Gathered to kill on the desolate plain

No fear in our minds

Pure hate in our hearts

Miscalculation of our strength their bane

Take us lightly and we'll make you pay

Pride left them defenseless

No mercy for hubris

They rush to fight us and we stand and wait

Pulses quicken as they take the bait

Mere seconds to slaughter

We can wait no longer

Closing fast with their weapons high

Still believing it's we that will die

Now the ambush is sprung

Now they learn they were wrong

Now the killing will start

Tear the bastards apart

They thought it would be easy but now they're being crushed

Arrogance of power leaves them dying in their blood

There will be no mercy for these filthy sons of whores

The innards of my enemies impaled upon my sword

Many years we've waited for this final day of slaughter

Our victims are decapitated, their limbs are torn asunder

Careful preparation brought our haughty victims down

Our forces are at full strength and the time to kill is now

Time to kill is now

Time to kill

They are all dead, it's their end today

All lost their lives in tremendous pain

Not one has survived

We left none alive

Do not doubt our conviction to kill

Hate on our side we will never fail

Now the killing will start

Tear the bastards apart

Strike the enemy down

The time to kill is motherfucking now!

ALEX WEBSTER

This song is quite literally about an ambush in a battle, which could have happened 1500 years ago or whatever. A force tricks their enemy into thinking that they're weaker than they actually are, and ambushes them. In addition to the literal meaning, I was thinking about our band a little bit when I wrote this, and how a lot of people had underestimated us. You get that feeling when you get terrible reviews in magazines, year after year, which we did an awful lot at the beginning of our career. You'd see comments online from people who didn't think the band was that good. If you look at really old reviews of Cannibal Corpse from the first five or six years of the band, we got really beat up by the press. When I wrote this song, Rob had just rejoined the band and our forces were at full strength. The song isn't literally about us, but it was on my mind that we had been underestimated a lot, and I was like "Now we're ready!" The vibe of the song was inspired by our situation at the time, even if the lyrics weren't.

MAKE THEM SUFFER

LYRICS: MAZURKIEWICZ · MUSIC: O'BRIEN

Suffer!

Extreme pain is what they need to feel for the rest of their lives

Misery and despair leaves their souls when infinity ends

Let them taste the wrath as the agony consumes them

Swallowed by the darkest light a blackened state of dismay

Survival is the only thing left for them

This grievous revelation is a new beginning

Led to the solution against their will

Deprivation thrives as the therapy continues

Sullen mastery is an answer uncontested

Denial is the only thing left for them

Life as they knew it is a distant memory

Scores of victims lust for apathy

Make them suffer

While they plead for cessation

Entirely demoralized and close to mass extinction

Damned to please supremacy

The reason for their martyrdom they will never know

Make them suffer

While they bleed through damnation

Begged for retribution before meeting with demise

Cursed by animosity

Once chosen for this mad ordeal there is no escape

Domination reigns supreme, the evil has no end
Spent of all their energy now worthless and degraded
Slow death is the only thing left for them
Physically and mentally devoid of dignity
Languished immortality

Make them suffer

While they plead for cessation
Entirely demoralized and close to mass extinction
Damned to please supremacy
The reason for their martyrdom they will never know

Make them suffer
While they bleed through damnation
Begged for retribution before meeting with demise
Cursed by animosity
Once chosen for this mad ordeal there is no escape

Make them suffer
Forever

PAUL MAZURKIEWICZ

This is one of my favorite Cannibal songs, and it's one of our most popular, too. Pat did a great job on the music. I wanted to write lyrics that were not R-rated or offensive, having written many songs that are extremely violent, and I think they worked out. It's not brutal in the way that some of our songs are brutal: this is me being vague about these people who end up being made to be miserable and they don't know why. Most people know why they're suffering: it's because someone hit you in the face, or because your dog died. These people have no idea why they're in pain. The video doesn't portray exactly what the lyrics are about, because we would have needed more people and more budget to make that happen, but it's still cool.

PAUL MAZURKIEWICZ

FROM BLIZZARDS TO BLASTBEATS, PAUL TELLS THE TALE
OF A QUARTER-CENTURY BEHIND THE DRUMS OF DOOM.

I was born on September 8, 1968, in Great Falls, Montana. My great-grandparents came from Poland: I'm 100 percent of Polish descent. My dad was in the US Air Force, so I was born on the base where my family was stationed for four years. I've never been back to Grand Falls, but nothing in Montana is that big. We've never even played in Montana! The whole family is really from Buffalo, though, where my younger sister was born after we moved back there when I was two years old.

My first memories would be from Buffalo, living there with my family and relations. Playing in the yard, doing things around the house... my sister and I grew up in the suburbs of Buffalo, and I had a fairly normal childhood. In first and second grade I went to Grover Cleveland Elementary School, which is still there. The schools there were named after presidents, so after that I went to Theodore Roosevelt and then Woodrow Wilson. I would have gone to John

F Kennedy but we moved. I got spanked by a teacher called Miss Moran once: I'm not sure if my parents ever knew that. I was a fairly decent student, though: I tried as hard as I could and I didn't get into much trouble.

Music came around when I was around nine years old, around 1977. I remember going through my dad's record collection. We weren't a big music family: my parents liked it, but it wasn't a huge part of their lives and they didn't play musical instruments. The first music that I found on my own was the Beach Boys. I was definitely into them. I really liked the Kinks too: my father had 'You Really Got Me' and 'All Day and All of the Night' on 45, and I loved them for some reason. Right off the bat I was interested in that gritty guitar sound. Back then they sounded pretty intense. They were a great band: really ahead of their time with a lot of their songs, although there was nothing visual there that grabbed me. That first happened with Kiss came around.

I have a cousin called Jerry Daminski who is two years older than me, and growing up he was like a brother to me. He contributed a lot to my musical background. He told me to check Kiss out—and I was blown away. I remember Kiss played in 1977 or '78 and I couldn't go to the show, so I cut out the clip from the paper the next day. I wasn't obsessed with them yet, just a little bummed that I didn't see the show.

As time passed, though, I got into them in a big way. The first album I ever bought at a record store was Destroyer. It changed my life. I lived Kiss and worshipped them from then on. I was the typical American 10-year-old who was witnessing Kiss at the height of their existence. They were the biggest thing in the world, visually as well as musically. I was into comic books and Star Wars too: I was religiously into the Marvel superheroes as well, Spider-Man in particular, so it all fed into the same obsession with fantasy. Gene Simmons was my idol.

By 1979, I'd been infatuated with Kiss for two years. I had Kiss plastered all over my bedroom walls and I had the albums and comics. I never painted my face, which is bizarre: I don't know why I didn't. But I did have tons of pictures and magazines. My parents were a little like, "What the hell is going on here?" which is understandable when you look back, because every Kiss song is about sex or partying. But I didn't know anything about that in 1979. For me it was about the music and what they looked like, not what they were talking about.

That year, I heard that Kiss were coming to Buffalo on the Dynasty tour. They were going to play at the Memorial Auditorium in Buffalo, where the Sabres hockey team played. I saw all my concerts there, growing up. I freaked out when I heard they were coming: nothing was gonna stop me seeing this one, having missed the earlier show. A friend told me his aunt would take us, so that was the plan, but that all fell apart just before the show and I was distraught: it really hit me that hard. My mom could see how important it was to me, so she went and bought tickets for the entire family to go to the show. It's so cool looking back at that. They didn't care about Kiss and nor did my sister: they did it for me.

The show was everything I thought it would be. I remember my parents had a good time: as we walked away, they told me that it had been a great show. Of course, how could it not be entertaining? I'm really glad they took me—because it was the start of it all for me.

By 1980 I had discovered Cheap Trick. I was hugely into them. I saw them in Buffalo, once each year in 1980 and '81. Around that time, I got knee-deep into music, and specifically heavy metal. The whole scheme of heavy music was starting to change: the mainstream started to get heavier.

An uncle named Matt married into my family: he was a drummer in a polka band. I remember seeing him play a couple of times. Every couple of years we'd go over to his house for my cousins' birthday party and they'd play music in a band called the Polecats. They'd set up in the garage and play for the family. I began to fixate on the drums at this point, because I could actually see them being played in front of me. There was more movement going on there than with any other instrument. I was still interested in the guitar, though, and in fact that became the first instrument I learned, when I was 12 or 13. I took lessons, and they're the only formal lessons I've ever taken. I went to an old-school music store and there was a young guy there who was giving lessons. I learned the notes and basic chords over a period of about six months. I look at the books now and I can't believe that I could read the notation: there's no way I could do that now.

Every day music was becoming more a part of my life. I wanted to plug in an electric guitar and play loud. My parents weren't going to buy me an electric guitar, though, because I was probably not going to study seriously—so in the end I lost interest in sitting there and strumming chords and gave it up. It wasn't until I was 15 that I got into the drums, so there was probably a period of three years where I didn't play any instrument.

I met Chris Barnes in middle school, in about 1981. He was heavily into Motörhead and turned me onto them. I then got into Rush and Black Sabbath. I bought Heaven and Hell when it came out, and I loved it and went back and got into older Sabbath, with Ozzy on vocals. When MTV came into play, it took music to a whole new level. I'm sure I watched it on the very first day it was on. I saw Iron Maiden opening for Judas Priest on the Screaming for Vengeance tour. The only song I knew by Priest was 'You've Got Another Thing Coming': I thought it was so brutal, which is funny when you look back at it now. I loved Number of the Beast by Iron Maiden. The cover was terrifying and amazing at the same time. I liked the earlier two Iron Maiden records too, which came out before Number of the Beast. The rawness of it all really blew my mind.

As time passed, my cousin Jerry got into drumming and even more into heavy metal. He got a new kit with double bass drums—a big, 12-piece, Neil Peart-style set—and I'd go over and sit behind the kit and go "Wow!" One day I picked up the sticks and hit a slow, 4/4 beat. I just did it, with no-one showing me how to do it. It turned out I had rhythm and a bit of timing, and I said to myself, "I can do this. I want to play drums."

So in 1985 I got my first drum kit. Thrash metal was around by this time, and we were growing with the music. At first it was a little weird: a friend of mine brought Metallica's Kill 'em All into school and said "Check this out." I bought a Music For Nations compilation called Hell on Earth with Manowar, Virgin Steele and Metallica on there, and the Metallica song was 'Metal Militia.' I didn't like it. It was hard for me to comprehend because I wasn't used to any speed picking. I was like, "What is this?" It was beyond me because it wasn't Priest, Sabbath or Maiden. Then I heard the rest of the album. 'Seek and Destroy' was a bit more of a traditional metal song, and I understood it a lot better, but I still wasn't fully there yet. Barnes had Slayer's Show No Mercy on cassette, and that was another level entirely. I didn't really like that either.

Months passed and our tastes evolved. I heard Metallica's Ride the Lightning and that set it off for me, right there. I wasn't a musician yet, I was just a metal fan, wearing the metal garb and wanting to hear the next heaviest thing. I'll never forget hearing 'Creeping Death' for the first time. We were home at my buddy Rich's house, where me and him and Barnes hung out for a couple of summers and religiously listened to metal, and the song came on the radio. We were like "Holy fuck, dude, what is this?" When we heard it was a song from the new Metallica album,

we flipped out. We were speechless. It was the heaviest thing we'd ever heard, so we went and got the album and that was it for me. It set me on a whole new path. 'Fight Fire With Fire' utterly blew me away. It freaked us out. We'd never felt this way about music before. It was a whole different ballgame now.

When we heard that Metallica were coming to Buffalo on the Ride the Lightning tour, we were like "Holy fuck!" We shit our pants and freaked out. So we got our tickets but we needed a ride, because none of us could drive yet. They were coming to Buffalo in January 1985, with WASP and Armored Saint, and Metallica were opening that night. It was a saloon bar they were playing in, an all-ages show, about 15 minutes away from where me and my friends lived.

So what happens? A big fuckin' blizzard hit Buffalo that day. We were like "You gotta be kidding me..." We didn't have a ride all day, and finally someone's dad said he'd give us a ride in his tiny Chevy Chevette. This car wasn't built for driving through snow, for sure. We were lucky we didn't get stuck in the snow, but we finally got to the show and there we were, in front of this band that we just worshiped.

The entire show, I stood in front of Kirk Hammett and I just headbanged. The whole time! I remember James Hetfield kicking over a glass in front of us, and I remember looking over at Cliff Burton on the other side. It was definitely the best thing I'd ever seen in my life up until this point. We couldn't believe that they were standing there, two feet in front of us. Afterwards I had to stay at my buddy's house for three whole days, because the entire city was shut down. For those three days, we were like, "We made it!"

When I finally met Metallica in 1992 and talked to them about it, Lars Ulrich

remembered that show, because the weather got so bad that they had difficulty getting out afterwards.

Chris and our friend Rich Ziegler and I got together in about 1985 and decided that we wanted to be in a band, although none of us could play anything at the time. I said I'd get a drum set and give it a go, having seen my cousin and uncle play, so I bought my first drum kit for 200 bucks. I remember I went with my mom to buy it: it was an old kit from the 60s. We shoved it into my mom's Pinto, which ended up being my first car after I got my driver's license.

I set up the kit in the basement and got started. I never had lessons: I didn't want anybody to show me, although I don't really understand now why I was like that. We were serious: we wanted to form a band. We didn't expect anything, because all we wanted to do was get together and make noise, so I learned a few songs and attempted to emulate them. Rich played bass, and Barnes became the singer because he wasn't a musician. We tried a few guitarists without getting much done, before we found Bob Rusay, who was in the grade above us at school.

The first song we ever tried was 'Pounding Metal' by Exciter, and Celtic Frost's 'Dethroned Emperor' was the second. We could play Slayer's 'Black Magic' because it has an easier riff, although we didn't do it very well at first. We tried Judas Priest and Accept songs too: it was basically a big mix of metal. Barnes wanted to sing, and he tried, but it wasn't good.

We called ourselves Obliviator. Our first gig might have been in late 1985 or early '86. I didn't get my first real kit until I graduated in late '86 and got a Tama Swingstar. We finally got a gig at a battle of the bands competition at a bar in Buffalo called the Salty Dog Skyroom Saloon. I still had my crappy kit so my cousin Jerry lent me his massive Neil Peart setup. I think we played six songs and we either won or came second, I can't remember. We did win two hours of studio time though. It was fun. We were still trying to find our identity. I remember we played at my grandfather's house for my graduation party. It was great! The family were all there.

Obliviator's first real gig, I guess, was a Halloween party in late 1986 where we were the entertainment. That was a little exciting. Barnes was out of the band at this point: we wanted to play Priest and Maiden songs, but he wasn't a singer, so he left. It was a mutual thing and he had another opportunity because Leviathan, another band from Buffalo, approached him. Leviathan were incredible: way ahead of their time. They were really precise musicians, which

had a real impact on us and really inspired us to do better. Seeing them, we realised what we could do.

We started to write some songs. Things started rolling once we had originals. They were heavy metal meets thrash: I was playing a few thrash beats but it was mostly mainstream metal until Slayer's Reign in Blood came out in 1987 and changed everyone, musically. I'll never forget it: I bought it at the mall and played it at home. That day changed my life. I knew we wanted to do something like that.

Our songs became more serious, and we changed our name to Tirant Sin, which I got from a short story in literature class in tenth grade. I ripped that page out from the book because it was so amazing and weird. We jammed in Rusay's basement, saved some money and recorded a four-song demo, although we still didn't have a singer so I sang two songs and Rich sang two. I think we hoped that the demo would attract a singer, which it did: the new guy was called Dennis, and he ended up singing on the second Tirant Sin demo.

Later, Barnes rejoined and we recorded a third demo, which was when we really started to get serious: we sent them to a few record labels and fanzines. That one was reviewed in Metal Forces in their demo column. Leviathan were in that issue too, talking about how Barnes had quit to rejoin Tirant Sin, and they appeared on the first Metal Forces compilation.

There had been a lot of progression among us in the year or two that Barnes was away in Leviathan. He was singing in a kind of thrash style, and we knew we didn't need a Rob Halford-style singer any more: we wanted a thrash guy, like Mille Petrozza of Kreator for example.

In May 1988 our guitar player quit, the day after a show with Beyond Death. We thought, "OK, we'll get another guitar player" and recruited Mike Green from Leviathan. He was a whole other level of guitarist, and he blew all of us away, although I'm not sure any of us were ready to play with a guy as good as that. Then Rich, our bass player, quit because he wasn't really into it any more—and that was the end of Tirant Sin.

Fortunately Alex called Bob and asked if we wanted to team up with him and Jack. Bob said yes. You know what we called our new band, of course.

DEATH WALKING TERROR

LYRICS AND MUSIC: WEBSTER

I am the black thoughts of the night
Deep in the darkness of your mind
Shrouded in shadow, the mental torture
In the realm of death walking terror

Stalking the closest to the edge
Imposition of depravity
Sanity holding by a thread
Desperation draws them close to me

Always unseen but never far behind
Fleeting darkness tricks your eyes
Paranoia, a creeping horror
Guided by the death walking terror

Your hand reaches for the knife
Subconscious molding insidious
It was always in your mind
Release the pain, a psychotic rush

Death walking terror
Slow mental torture

I am the blood you seek to spill
I am your inner drive to kill
Dark inspiration, a moral failure
Created by the death walking terror

Your hands have done my bidding well
Your hideous dreams now reality
Manipulation done with stealth
I was with you, I heard the screams

Death walking terror
Slow mental torture
Death walking terror
Psychic tormentor

The weakest ones will fall
My murderous influence appeals to their fear
My will is just too strong
The decision was mine but they'll never know

Death walking terror

I walk behind you while you kill
Usurping your mind, you are oblivious
You'll never know your spirit fell
Supplanted by this deep disgust

Death walking terror, slow mental torture
Death walking terror, psychic tormentor

ALEX WEBSTER

The tempo of this song is at a walking pace, but at a menacing speed, striding with a killer's confidence towards you. We had started using lower tuning a lot more when I wrote this song: we were going down three steps, or a minor third, for each string, and that tuning works really well for slower songs. I like grooves that are around this speed, which is probably about 90bpm.

This song is about someone following a guy, like a devil on his shoulder making him kill. We had a great video made for it by a guy named Dan Dobi: he had done a great job on the 'Make Them Suffer' video, although the content of that video didn't really have a lot to do with the lyrics of the song. With 'Death Walking Terror', though, I got together with Dan beforehand, went through the lyrics with him and asked him to tie in the visuals more closely with them. It's the most effective video that we've ever done: it's really creepy. Everything came together on this song: the music, the lyrics and the video. It's a popular song for us, and it works really well in contrast to the faster songs which we play live.

PRIESTS OF SODOM

LYRICS AND MUSIC: WEBSTER

The blackened city calls out
Enter the temple of sin
You must enter the temple of sin
Contorted sinners beckon
Join our twisted rites
You must join our twisted rites

The priests' eyes gleam
Blood on their scepters of flesh
There is blood on their scepters of flesh
The nubile virgin bows
Await the piercing thrust
She awaits the piercing thrust
Perverse rites

Priests of Sodom preside
We are damned
Praise the gods of sin
Her walls are burning
Grinding the staff of the priest
Sluts grinding the staff of the priest
The congregation
Revel in sins of the flesh
They revel in sins of the flesh

Whores from the temple
Serving shamanic desire
They are serving shamanic desire
Deviant bodies writhing

Slick with the fluids of lust
They are slick with the fluids of lust
Perverse rites

Priests of Sodom preside
We are damned
Immortal lust
Wicked legions come forth
Defile the pure
Statues of demons glisten with sweat
The orgy intensifies violence begins
Flagellate sluts with serpentine whips
They raise their blades to throats of their men
Climax approaches and the blood will spill
Sexual sacrifice, mutilation and death
Murder

Priests of Sodom
Priests of Sodom
Priests of Sodom
Priests of Sodom
Priests of Sodom
Perverse rites

Priests of Sodom preside
We are damned
Immortal lust
Wicked legions come forth
Defile the pure

ALEX WEBSTER

Sodom is a real place as far as we know, but in my depiction I'm thinking of something like the orgy scenes in Conan the Barbarian. At the time when I wrote this, there was that whole Catholic priests scandal going on, and although it has absolutely nothing to do with that, a whole lot of people were like, "Cannibal are criticizing the Catholic church and that scandal!" There were men that functioned as priests around long before any of the modern religions, of course, and Sodom was around thousands of years before Christ, so the song has nothing to do with any current events. It's strictly a fictionalized tale of perversions and atrocities that were going on in some city from ancient times.

In general, I would like Cannibal Corpse to be a band that takes you away from reality, which is why I would rather not comment in a song on real-life events or issues. I don't mind if other bands do it, but for me, I'd rather stay away. That's just my personal viewpoint.

CARNIVOROUS SWARM

LYRICS: MAZURKIEWICZ · MUSIC: O'BRIEN ·

Stain the sky, Armageddon
Dormant mass now awakened
Summoned fury devastation
Enormous force annihilates
All that breathes shall be engulfed
Within its path, everything dies
Ravage the earth, conquer its life

Here to devour
Vicious attack, ferociously savage
Beyond a primal desire
Horde of the apocalypse arrives
Bombardment from oblivion, invading legion gorges
Eradicate through infestation
Horde of the apocalypse destroys
Strike begins, it is a battle that is one-sided
Swarm consumes
Droves assail, congregation with aggressive nature
Swarm of death kills

Stain the sky, Armageddon
Dormant mass now awakened
All that breathes shall be engulfed
Within its path everything dies
Ravage the earth, conquer its life
Here to devour

Vicious attack, ferociously savage
Beyond a primal desire
Horde of the apocalypse arrived
Bombarded from oblivion, invading legion gorged
Eradicated through infesting
Horde of the apocalypse destroyed
Strike begins, it was a battle that is one-sided
Swarm consumes
Droves assail, congregation with aggressive nature

Swarm of death kills
Ravage the earth, conquer its life
Here to devour
Vicious attack, ferociously savage
Beyond a primal desire

PAUL MAZURKIEWICZ
The riff here sounds like a swarm of bees, so it made sense to come up with a title that reflected that sound. I wanted it to sound prehistoric, like "Here's some horrifying bugs! They're going to kill everything!"

DEMENTED AGGRESSION

LYRICS: MAZURKIEWICZ · MUSIC: O'BRIEN

Pain is my reward from psychotic tendencies
Pain I give to you
Pain relentlessly
Torturing has reached a level no-one's ever seen
Suffer for your life
Rabid force extreme
Rage is my obsession driven by my cruelty
Rage is my release
Rage relentlessly
Ravaging continues through my scattered lunacy
Malice for your life
Rapid force extreme

Demented aggression

Hate is the reason I embrace these fantasies
Hate engulfs my mind
Hate relentlessly
With pain and rage and hatred relentlessly

With pain
Rage and hate
Beatings come faster
Beatings last longer
With pain
Rage and hate
Beatings are forever
I don't think you'll live
I don't think you'll live

Don't think you'll live
Don't think you'll live
I don't think you'll live

Pain is my reward from psychotic tendencies

Rage is my release
Hate relentlessly
With pain and rage and hatred relentlessly

With pain
Rage and hate
Torture coming faster
Torture lasting longer
With pain
Rage and hate
Torture is forever
I don't think you'll live
I don't think you'll live

Don't think you'll live
Don't think you'll live
I don't think you'll live

Left as a pummeled mound of waste
Rot and decay under the sun

With pain
Rage and hate
Suffering is faster
Suffering is longer
With pain
Rage and hate
Suffering is forever
I don't think you'll live
I don't think you'll live

PAUL MAZURKIEWICZ
I mixed it up a little on this song, and I really liked the way it turned out. Pat did a great job. Notice that I didn't want there to be any specific killing mentioned: there might be some death, but you're not sure. You'll get beaten down by all this rage and hate and you might not live. If you don't, whatever, but if you do, you're gonna be hurting. I think the line being repeated adds a lot of power. It's typical of my recent writing style in that it's obvious what's happening: you don't need to decipher a metaphor to figure it out.

AS DEEP AS THE KNIFE WILL GO

LYRICS: MAZURKIEWICZ · MUSIC: O'BRIEN

The blade goes in you and it enters smooth
Disturbing moans begin to soothe
Scraping bones with steel to feel it once
Keep pushing hard it never stops

Had to do it
Had to put it in your gut
Nothing to it
Grab the handle let it slice
Heart polluted
As it's cut out of your chest
Gushing fluids
Bleeding it dry

As deep as the knife will go
A life-changing transfer of power
As deep as the knife will go

As deep as the knife will go
Every inch of it in you savored
As deep as the knife will go

The blade has always done its job well
Seems like its work is never done
Scraping bone with steel to feel it twice
Keep pushing hard it doesn't stop

Desecrated
A body rid of living
Future faded

Gaping hole from front to back
Heart dissected
As it sits upon your chest
Gushing fluids
Drain you empty

As deep as the knife will go
A life-changing transfer of power
As deep as the knife will go

As deep as the knife will go
Every inch of it in you savored
As deep as the knife will go

Bleed it dry
Bleed it dry
Drain you empty
Drain you empty

Bleed it dry
Bleed it dry
Drain you empty
Drain you empty

As deep as the knife will go
A life-changing transfer of power
As deep as the knife will go

As deep as the knife will go
Every inch of it in you savored
As deep as the knife will go

PAUL MAZURKIEWICZ

"A life-changing transfer of power..." The title of this song was gold as soon as we saw it, and I wanted the lyrics to be obvious. It's about somebody who has never held a knife in their hand and put it into somebody, let alone actually killed someone. That's the whole story right there: the person isn't necessarily supposed to be a bad person, but he still did it, for whatever reason, even though he didn't mean to. It still happened, and the person is changed afterwards, because the life is drained from the dead person and goes into the killer. What's more, he loved it!

FOLLOWED HOME THEN KILLED

LYRICS: MAZURKIEWICZ · MUSIC: O'BRIEN

Creeping in the shadows
Shadows of the night
Wading through the darkness
A death before the light
Blending in with faces
Faces of the night
Safe at home in comfort
At home is where you'll die

Watching you
Knowing your every move
Hearing you
Every single word that you spew
Carving you
Is what I'm about to do
Saving you
From the torment of this earth to be buried for rebirth

Silently I enter through the broken basement window now to wait
It's twelve o'clock the time has come to ascend the staircase to the hunted one
Make way to the second floor right outside your open bedroom door
One last time to sleep in peace unaware of brutal things that

Will be done
To you after you wake
Enter slow
Machete leads the way
Eerie calm
Death is in the air

Savage thrust

Death is everywhere

Adrenaline is pumping as my heart is pounding faster than yours slows down

Choke on blood and breathe your last breath mangled

Guts I wear to celebrate

Stay inside and fuck the corpse, an innards orgy satisfies my needs

Finally I feel complete by eating brains and flesh

Followed home then killed

Sacrificed in vain

Followed home then killed

I stalked you for years

Followed home then killed

Take what's left in garbage bags and throw them in a hole I dug out back

Clean the room I killed you in, making sure the clues of sin are gone

Revel in my vicious deed and replay what happened in my head

Vivid memories of you remain of your remains

Followed home then killed

Sacrificed in vain

Followed home then killed

I stalked you for years

Followed home then killed

Followed home then killed

PAUL MAZURKIEWICZ

Pat loved this title as soon as he heard it. My inspiration was old-school, early-80s horror films. It reminds you of our old songs, off Eaten Back to Life. It's basic: someone gets stalked and then killed in their own house. Like Last House on the Left, perhaps. Compare this to 'Perverse Suffering', which was the first song I wrote for Cannibal: it had all these big words in it because I felt I needed them. I'm glad I got out of that mindset. I really like the way I write now, and I'm sure it's the way I'll keep writing in the future.

PART 2:
A BRIEF HISTORY OF MURDER, MAYHEM AND MISANTHROPY

CANNIBAL CORPSE'S GRUESOME FIRST 25 YEARS,
TOLD BY THE MUSICIANS WHO LIVED IT —
AND SURVIVED TO TELL THE TALE

The story of Cannibal Corpse as a band began in 1989, after a debut show at Buffalo's River Rock Café in April in support of Dark Angel. Deciding to focus on horror themes, the band swiftly gained an identity quite separate from the Satanic and occult songwriting practiced by many other death metal bands of the day.

Alex I just didn't believe in Satanism. There were enough bands doing the Satanic thing, and they seemed committed to it, but I wanted to do something else. In the 80s, death metal, black metal and some of the darker thrash metal bands were almost all the same, really: it's like a tree in which the branches become more distinct as they get further from the trunk, but they all started from the same root. Look at Sepultura: they started out as a death metal band with Satanic lyrics, and became a thrash band.

I liked the lyrics from Death's *Scream Bloody Gore* album: although I didn't know all the lyrics or even have a lyric sheet, I knew from song titles like 'Baptized in Blood' and 'Regurgitated Guts' that they were a gore band. The imagery was great. Necrophagia was another band that had some good gore/horror lyrics, and they were clearly a death metal band. Together with the band name that I came up with, and all the crazy cannibal films that we liked, we thought that should be the focus. Cannibal Corpse was a reanimated body which consumes other humans: the theme of the band was spelled out for us right there.

I wanted the lyrics to be genuinely frightening. I wanted our songs to scare people, like a great horror film or book from the 70s. The lyrics need to be surreal, because what frightens people is when something weird happens that is not like reality. Like in the movie *Phantasm*, when the guy bleeds yellow blood. Sometimes things that don't make sense are the scariest. For example, in *The Shining*, there's a part where you see a guy in a bear suit giving a blowjob to a guy in a tuxedo. You're like, "What the fuck is that?" It's terrifying because it's so weird.

After recording a five-song demo tape and sending it to various record companies, Brian Slagel of Metal Blade signed Cannibal up. They're still there, 25 years later.

Brian Slagel Cannibal sent us a demo cassette, and the first thing I did was look at the song titles. There was a song on there called 'A Skull Full Of Maggots,' and I immediately thought that I should sign this band based on that song title alone! The demo turned out to be really good, and we ended up signing them in 1989. There were other death metal bands around— Morbid Angel, Death, Obituary and so on—and some of those bands were writing gory lyrics, but no other band was doing that to this extreme, that's for sure. I always thought that was really cool: that the lyrics were so over the top. The music was really good too, which was great because you can't just have bizarre song titles: there has to be musical quality as well. They were in their late teens, I think, when they sent the demo to us, but the musicianship was pretty good for the time. It was raw, but it was really good, and you could see that there was a lot of potential there. Cannibal had the whole package.

Chris was the first guy we spoke to, and after that it was Chris plus Alex and Paul. They had no management for the longest time, but those guys were pretty smart, which made me feel good when I spoke to them because they weren't just some dumb kids. Overall, they've been the easiest band on the label to deal with: there's never been a problem. I think we've had maybe one disagreement in all the years we've been together! They get the business, they understand it, and the relationship between us and them works very smoothly.

On August 17, 1990, *Eaten Back to Life* was released.

Alex On *Eaten Back To Life*, Chris did most of the lyrics. We were all into horror movies, and so were most of the guys on the scene, but maybe Chris was into them a little bit more. He was good at writing lyrics and he really wanted to focus on them. It was his job. We were fine with that, but by the time we were getting ready to do *Created to Kill*, which became *Vile*, I asked if I could help write some lyrics and he said "Sure" and I started writing lyrics for the song 'Bloodlands.'

We try to have a balance between obscure, spooky music and really pounding, caveman stuff. The more straightforward stuff is placed on the first half of the albums, so that people's interest is retained long enough to draw them into the deeper cuts, shall we say. The lyrics go that way too: a hugely important part of Cannibal Corpse is the caveman songs, with the Neanderthal, pounding-your-head-in sound, and we combine those with the more experimental songs—and I feel that's part of the reason for our success.

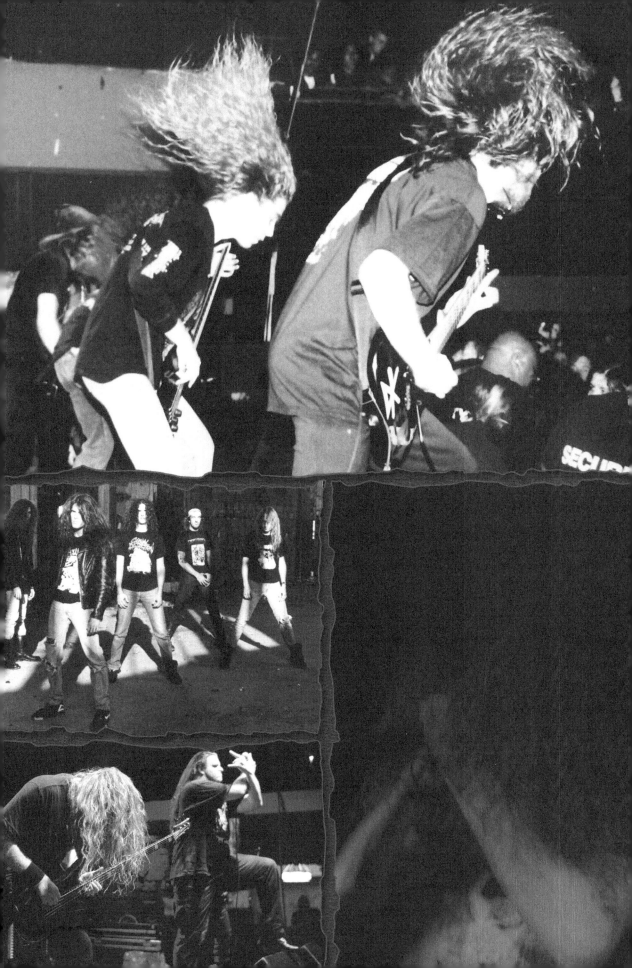

We don't have just one sound. It's all about horror and it's all death metal, but there's quite a bit of variety within those parameters. I always thought visuals were more horrific than lyrics, myself. When you see an eyeball get skewered by a piece of broken wood in a Lucio Fulci movie, there's much more impact than having that described in words.

Soon afterwards, Cannibal hit the road.

Paul I remember we were playing a big festival with Immolation and Mortician at the Skyroom in 1990. The sister of my girlfriend at the time was a bit of a psycho, and hit another girl in the face during our set, as we found out afterwards. The second girl was obviously very upset and her boyfriend ended up throwing a set of heavy vinyl stickers in my face, right in front of everyone. Apparently it was my fault that my girlfriend's sister was insane and punched his girlfriend. We ended up fighting and people pulled us apart.

Alex We were thrust into a headlining situation almost immediately, because there weren't a whole lot of bands to open for back then. Within a few albums we were playing live sets that lasted over an hour, and by the time we were into the new millennium we were mostly playing at least 75 minutes in our headlining set. We learned quickly that to make a really interesting set, it helps to have songs at various tempos, as long as they're all heavy. If you play 75 minutes of jackhammer high-speed metal, it takes away the impact of that speed, but if you have a slow song and then follow it with something really fast, it's a great contrast. The slow songs sound heavier and the fast songs sound more aggressive.

In 1991, Cannibal's lyrics and cover artwork became more graphic with their second album, *Butchered at Birth*, released on July 1.

Brian Slagel The first salvo of controversy around Cannibal Corpse started around the *Butchered at Birth* album. People knew about the band already, of course, because they already had the first record out, which itself was pretty extreme. At the time we were distributed by Warner Brothers, but we felt that *Butchered* would be a little too much for them, so we kept the album out of the Warners deal and distributed it independently. It was cooler to do it that way anyway.

When we got the album artwork in, some of the people at the label were concerned about it and asked me "What do you think of this? It's pretty extreme" but I said "It's one of the greatest album covers I've ever seen!" I knew it was going to attract a lot of attention out there, but I've always liked to push the envelope. I grew up being a huge Alice Cooper and Kiss fan, and I knew it would make an impact.

Alex Would you want to live in a world where people couldn't make art that was ugly? I say no. We're very clear in all the interviews we do that these are just fictional horror stories, and that these are not characters which we relate to. One of the reasons we've had such problems with censorship is that people look at movies and they say, "Eli Roth made *Hostel* and he clearly does not think that people should be taken into a Slovakian factory and tortured to death for money." If we write a song about the same thing, people go, "Most of the songs I've listened to throughout my life are guys singing about their girlfriends and how much they love them" and they assume that we're coming from the same standpoint as musicians, but we're not. We're approaching our lyrics the way a horror movie is approached. Or a novel by Stephen King: there's all sorts of violence in those books, but no-one thinks any less of him because of it.

Perhaps the most extreme songs written in the Chris Barnes era came from 1992's *Tomb of the Mutilated* album, released on September 22. These included 'Necropedophile' and 'Entrails Ripped From a Virgin's Cunt'.

Alex 'Entrails' is so over the top that it's ridiculous. In our twenties, we weren't thinking too seriously about this stuff. Chris wrote the lyrics and we gave him free rein to be as offensive and disturbing as he thought necessary. Nowadays we probably think a little more about the subject matter of our songs, and the end result can be lyrics that are still horrifying but less overtly offensive. I think that sometimes a more subtle approach can be more effective for horror fiction anyway—'subtle' being a very relative term in our case, maybe the difference between a hatchet to the genitals and a hatchet to the head. But that's what our band is doing really: putting horror fiction to music. We don't back what the characters in our songs are doing: they're just evil characters who are appropriate for stories like these.

Paul When we were touring Germany with Sinister in October 1992, we had a day off in Nuremberg and we met these two girls. They were cool and wanted to hang out, and one of the girls worked in a bar and wanted to take us there. She drove us there and we ordered a giant bowl of alcohol with straws for everyone, which we sucked down in about fucking 10 seconds. It was called Dracula's Blood.

I was so hammered that I passed out with my head on the table. We ended up getting a ride back to the bus and I threw up profusely before I got in my bunk and slept for 12 hours solid. The next day I felt so sick and dehydrated, I think I actually had alcohol poisoning. Even though I'd slept for 12 hours, I had to go and lie down in a fetal position. I was so miserable, but I couldn't sleep. I lay there for about two hours, sweating. Finally I got up, drank some water in the bathroom and threw it up again immediately. This was my rock bottom! Eventually I managed to eat some bread and we played the show, although I don't know how I did it. I think it was pure adrenaline. I never got that wasted again after that.

Alex I got wasted on that same stuff with Dimebag Darrell on the same tour. Me, Bart and Mike from Sinister went out in Hamburg, where we'd played that night, and we went to the Reeperbahn, the red light district. We knew that Megadeth and Pantera had played a club called the Docks there that night, and we went to a Burger King. Who do we see but Dimebag Darrell and Nick Menza, plus a couple of their crew?

I was wearing a Butchered at Birth T-shirt, and Dimebag asked me where I got it. I told him I was in the band and he seemed really excited: he said he'd been driving around with friends in Dallas and one of them had played our music for him. He thought it was really crazy and over the top and invited us to go party with him. So we went to a bar and drank that Dracula's Blood and a whole bunch of other drinks. We had a really great night with him: he was one of the nicest guys we ever met. We met Dimebag again when we were in Japan in 1996, although I'm not sure how much he remembered of that time in Hamburg.

1993 was a turbulent year for Cannibal Corpse, with Bob Rusay dismissed from the band. His replacement was Malevolent Creation guitarist Rob Barrett. On March 23 the song 'Hammer Smashed Face' was released as an EP: it went on to become one of Cannibal's signature songs. The band's touring profile leaped a notch after two high-profile jaunts through Europe with acts such as Carcass, Tiamat, Gorefest, Death (the Full Of Hate tour) and Desultory, Hypocrisy, Fear Factory Sleep, Penance and Cathedral (Cannibal's headline tour).

Non-metal fans were introduced to Cannibal Corpse in 1994 via an unforgettable cameo in the Jim Carrey film *Ace Ventura: Pet Detective*, performing a chunk of 'Hammer Smashed Face'. Seeing is believing...

Brian Slagel Somebody within the *Ace Ventura* movie got hold of the band, because Jim Carrey was a huge Cannibal Corpse fan, and said "We'd like to have you in this movie—what do you guys think?" The band contacted me and asked me what I thought, but I wasn't sure. They were such a cool underground band with a great vibe, and if you're in a mainstream movie it might make you seem less cool. So I was on the fence, because no-one knew who Jim Carrey was at the time, and it didn't seem like the movie was going to be that big.

In the end I said, "I guess it will probably be all right, if you want to do it." They said they did want to do it, so they went down there and did their thing. Before they went, they sent me a script, which I thought was terrible, but I thought "What the hell, it's fun for them: they get to be on a movie set for a couple of days." I thought it would all be forgotten really quickly. Then the producer called me up and invited me to a test screening in Los Angeles, which I was dreading, because I knew I was going to have to sit next to the producer and the director and say, "Yes, this is good!"... but I watched it and it was brilliant. Only Jim Carrey could make a script like that come off and be so amazing. Being in that film really took Cannibal to another level, because so many people saw them in it who never would have been exposed to them otherwise.

Alex Jim Carrey had bought a few of our albums, having seen the sleeves and thought, "What the fuck is this?" Then he took them home and found himself liking the music. So, when they needed a scene in the film where people are slam-dancing in a club, he

CAUTION
RESTRICTED NOISE AREA
ALL PERSONNEL WITHIN
THIS AREA MUST WEAR
APPROVED EAR MUFFS OR
EAR PLUGS

asked for us. He actually requested two specific songs—'Hammer Smashed Face' and 'Rancid Amputation.' We each got $450, plus everybody in the club got $50. We also get publishing royalties every time the movie is played, so since then we've each made a few thousand dollars. A cheque arrives from the Screen Actor's Guild from time to time—it's always a nice surprise.

After a spring European tour with Morbid Angel, US dates with Cynic and Sinister followed.

Alex I remember touring with Cynic and Sinister in the United States in 1994. We thought Cynic were fucking amazing. We had a day off in Texas, and we were driving all day between shows, with a stop scheduled somewhere. I really liked hanging out with Cynic, because we were friends with them since way back. In 1987 when Malevolent Creation moved to Fort Lauderdale from Buffalo, we stayed in contact with those guys. They met Cynic, who were from Miami, and later on both bands came up and did the Cynical Creation tour in 1989. They and Malevolent did a show with us at an Elk's Lodge in Buffalo, and another in downstate New York with Prime Evil. They also played a show at the River Rock Café a week later to replace Gwar, who had canceled a scheduled show. So we got to know Cynic. They were great guys.

Us and Sinister were a perfect match because we play a very similar style of death metal, so Cynic were sandwiched in there. They had some tough nights, because the fans didn't want to see progressive death metal: they wanted straightforward death metal. But we had nothing but the highest regard for them as musicians and as people. We would drink with them and watch movies together. They had a great sense of humour.

I remember that night, when we were driving across Texas, for some reason the only thing we had to drink was fucking Zima, which is an alcopop. We didn't have any beer, but the Zima had alcohol in it so we still had a good time. They were a great band to tour with.

On April 12, 1994, *The Bleeding* was released, followed up by more dates in America with Samael and Grave and a European run with Desultory and Samael once again.

Paul We were in Enschede, a little town in Holland, in 1994, on tour with a couple of bands. We're sharing a bus: there's three bands and crew on this vehicle, parked outside the club. It's midnight and everyone's gone home, and I see a little food stand open just down the road. Me and Barnes bought some food and took it to the bus to eat. Suddenly he goes, "Dude, there's fighting out there!" and we ran outside.

Alex Some drunks—not guys who had been at the show, just locals—were having words with our tour manager Doug Goodman for some reason, and then our soundman ran up and put one of them in a full nelson, because they were starting to get physical with Doug. It quickly devolved into a brawl and we paired off. I was fighting with some guy who was bigger and older than me. I wasn't much of a fighter back then, but I had spirit, so we were rolling around fighting pretty hard, and so was our soundman Paul Babikian. Our merch guy and Barnes came out and helped, and it got broken up. We had 22 people on this bus, so we had them outnumbered pretty quick.

Paul There was a lot of yelling in Dutch and German going on. Suddenly everybody started flying at each other, and this huge melee started. I was just watching in disbelief when I looked to my left, and there was this dude lunging at me, going "Aaaaagh!" He hit me in my side, and I was like "Holy shit, that hurt!" and I looked down and I was bleeding out of my side. At first I thought I just got kicked, but then I thought "If I was kicked, I wouldn't have a fucking puncture wound. I've been stabbed." So this fight's going on, but I don't remember exactly what happened because I staggered off towards the club. I do remember that Andy, our shirts guy, really beat the shit out of somebody.

Alex It's hard to remember, because I was dealing with my own situation, but Andy really took care of business. He was pretty tough: a regular-sized guy, but he knew what to do out there. He put his fingers in the eyes of the guy who was wrestling with me, and I think he kicked some other dudes with the cowboy boots he was wearing. Later on he told me, "I saw that fingers-in-the-eyes thing on TV. It really works!"

Paul So at this point I've got a wound and I'm bleeding. I'm going into shock, because it hurts, and I don't know if I'm going to collapse in the next 10 seconds because I've got something stuck in me. After a couple of minutes I realized I wasn't going to die, so some girl walked me into the club and they called an ambulance. I went to the hospital and they checked me out: it turned out the guy was holding some keys in his knuckles when he punched me, which made a hole. They said it was superficial and that I didn't need a stitch, so they just disinfected it and put a butterfly dressing on it. It hurt like fuck though, because it wasn't just a hole: an actual chunk of flesh had been torn out. My bunk was really hard to climb into as well, and I was in utter pain when I tried to get into it.

After an Australian tour in 1995, the biggest upheaval of Cannibal Corpse's career so far came when Chris Barnes was replaced in October by George Fisher, recently of Monstrosity. Recording sessions for the next album, *Created to Kill*, continued with George's new vocal tracks. The album was retitled *Vile* and became the first, but by no means the last, Cannibal Corpse album to hit the Billboard charts.

Alex We'd seen George play with Monstrosity, and thought he was a cool, funny guy, so we asked him to come down for *Vile*. He loves to sing, and he can belt the lyrics out at high speed, which was exactly what we wanted him to do.

Brian Slagel The one moment where Cannibal and I didn't agree was when they replaced Chris. At that point the band was getting really huge, and their next record could potentially have been massive, so the last thing you do in that situation is replace your frontman. But they did—and they didn't tell me about it, because they knew I wasn't going to be very happy! They said, "Oh, by the way, we did this" and I was like, "What? You did *what?*" I was pretty freaked out about it, but George turned out to be an incredible frontman and singer, and they didn't miss a beat. He's the perfect guy for them. Very few bands have been able to replace their frontman and remain successful: AC/DC is the only example I can think of. But it worked out fine for Cannibal—and we ended up with two bands, because we signed Chris's new band, Six Feet Under.

In a you-couldn't-make-it-up turn of events, Cannibal Corpse's name was mentioned in the corridors of power when the US Senator Bob Dole mentioned them in a list of acts who were supposedly engaged in "undermining the national character of the United States." The following is an excerpt from the *LA Times* of June 25, 1995, written by journalist Jonathan Gold:

Jonathan Gold I know Cannibal Corpse. In fact, I'm listening to the group's CD right now. It's pretty much a one-note band. Most of the songs on its first album seem to be about exhuming dead bodies, but then the group is working the highly regimented heavy-metal subgenre sometimes known as Grossout Metal. And that's an element that occupies about the same place in teenage culture as the dead-baby jokes that hormonally challenged 14-year-olds used to tell each other in the 60s.

But I wouldn't be listening to Cannibal Corpse today if Sen. Bob Dole hadn't blasted the group, among other entertainment entities, for "undermining the character of the nation"... A spokesman for Sen. Dole has admitted that the venerable legislator never actually listened to any of the records involved, even the popular ones, though he had studied the lyric sheets. If the senator *had* bothered to slap on a Cannibal Corpse CD, this is what he would have heard: "Wuh-wuh-wuh-wuh BLARGH wuh-wuh-wuh-wuh-wuhhhh." Actually, he probably would have heard even less than that, unless his speakers were really good. But, hey! Now the band is famous... if I were Cannibal Corpse, I'd be sending the senator a fruit basket right about now.

Brian Slagel There have been several interesting watershed moments for Cannibal over the years that really got them out in front. The Bob Dole thing was unbelievable. We'd been through the whole PMRC thing in the 80s, so we were pretty used to having government people saying nasty things about metal bands, but that really backfired on them because all it did was give the bands concerned huge amounts of publicity.

That's exactly what happened here. When that whole thing hit, the first thing we knew was that Chris Barnes was talking to Tom Brokaw on the national six o'clock news on NBC! Back then, millions and millions of people were watching the NBC news, and it was awesome, quite honestly. We couldn't be happier. All of a sudden stores started carrying Cannibal albums that wouldn't before.

Alex I was told that we were on a list of certain bands that Bob Dole mentioned. Of those bands, we were the smallest, and also one of the only bands that wasn't a hip-hop act. The cynical part of me thinks that we were put in there so the Republicans, who are viewed as racist by some, wouldn't be seen to be attacking only black artists. But that is speculation on my part.

I did find it interesting that around the same time, the 700 Club, led by the conservative pastor Pat Robertson, mentioned us alongside very similar bands. It makes me wonder if Bob Dole had actually done any research. I highly doubt he did. Why would a guy in his sixties care about this stuff? He had clearly been handed this list by somebody.

We're quite well protected by the laws in the United States: it's really quite a free place, although a lot of American citizens don't share that view. Cannibal Corpse has never had censorship problems from the government. The only problems of that nature that we've had have come from record stores who were scared to have our albums in their store, which is why we've sometimes done dual album covers to get our CDs into bigger chains. Stores like that would never have covers like *Butchered at Birth* just sitting there in plain view, so they pre-empted it for fear of what their customers would say.

In this band, the members either have different political views or are apathetic towards politics. There are enough bands who cover politics well and we've never felt the need to do that. There are a couple of songs which very briefly and vaguely allude to politics: 'Put Them to Death' is about executing criminals for their crimes, and 'Sentenced to Burn' is basically a song about how people are misled by demagogues. We don't have a consensus in this band about capital punishment: I'm ambivalent about it myself.

The same year, Cannibal Corpse found themselves under attack once again by a pack of politicians. A campaign by Senator Joe Lieberman, Senator Sam Nunn and others was attempting to persuade major record labels to drop a group of 20 bands who, they frothed, were responsible for offensive lyrics. It failed.

Alex Joe Lieberman mentioned us too. It's awesome publicity for us, especially in

America. They've never been able to harm us in a tangible way, whether by banning a show or an album. But in Europe, governments get involved.

More important things were on Cannibal's collective mind in '96, when tours through Europe took place alongside Immolation, Vader, Impaled Nazarene, Grave, Krabathor, Rotting Christ and Dark Tranquility. George had debuted with Cannibal at two shows with Kreator in Florida. Debauchery inevitably followed.

Alex I don't get drunk all that much, so when I do it's usually pretty special and people tend to remember it. We were on a bus, touring with Vader and Immolation: we'd just played in Rome on the first European tour we did with George in the band. We'd done a couple of American shows with Kreator to warm up, one in West Palm Beach and one in Orlando, and those were our first two shows with George. It was a great tour and we were having a great time.

George was much more outgoing with the fans than Chris had been, and I was really happy about that sort of thing. I was feeling really good about the situation and one night they gave us this case of beer on our rider – but it wasn't just any beer, it was this case of litre bottles of Heineken. They were really big: fucking huge, actually. They were cold and it was warm outside that day, so suddenly we started drinking a lot. There we were, us and Vader and Immolation, just loving life and happy. We were finally happy with the band: we were all getting along great and having a blast with our death metal brothers. I was psyched to be jamming with my band and I was toasting everyone.

George I'll never forget: Alex said to me, "Fuck yeah! I'm so glad you're in the band and I'm having fun again—and it's all because you came into the band." I remember it because it was a big deal.

Alex I was so stoked. With all due respect to Chris, from a musical and personal standpoint there had been problems. Anyway I was getting really fucking drunk, and all of a sudden I was in the bathroom throwing up. I don't know what happened next, but I woke up the next day in my bunk, or maybe in the middle of the floor of the bus, and I remember thinking, "I need some details here. What the fuck happened last night?" I asked the Immolation guys what happened and they said, "Dude, you were having the best time!"

The previous time I got super-drunk was after an Agnostic Front show, and I passed out with my contact lenses in, and woke up with pus all over my eyes. I had to go to the doctor and wear glasses for a week, putting in eyedrops for my infected eyes. This time, I couldn't find my contact lenses anywhere, and the Immolation guys told me that the night before, while the bus was rolling and I was completely hammered, somehow I got the lenses out of my eyes, put them away and did all that stuff in a completely inebriated state.

It was one of those nights that you remember—a big party night at a pivotal point on an important tour in our history. That whole tour was a big metal brotherhood and it's a great memory, even though I don't remember an hour or two of that night. The next day we played a show at a place called the Poison Apple in Torino, Italy, and I was so hungover that day. There's actually a promo picture of us that was taken that day at the Poison Apple, and George hates that picture because he'd accidentally put half of his hair back for that shot, so it looks a little weird. But I like it because it reminds me of a really killer night.

To celebrate the release of *Vile* on May 21, a VHS recording titled *Monolith of Death Tour 96-97* appeared in late 1996. Japanese and American dates with bands such as Anthrax, Brutal Truth and Immolation ensured that Cannibal's profile remained high. However, Rob left the band in 1997 to rejoin his old band Malevolent Creation: his replacement was sometime Nevermore axeman Pat O'Brien. The new arrival attracted a few interesting stalkers...

Pat There was this one girl who drove all over Europe, following me. She'd been around since the Nevermore days. I remember we saw her passed out in her car once. Nothing major happened between us, though.

Alex We're not the kind of band that a ton of women come to see. People come to our shows because they actually like the music. They're not here because they think we're good-looking. There were a few girls who showed up to connect with us on a romantic level, but there weren't very many of them—and those that came for that reason had connected with a lot of guys before us! It was the same dozen girls around the world that you'd see hanging around.

No stranger to the bottle, Pat enjoyed his time on the road to the maximum, often aided and abetted by his partner-in-crime George.

George One time, Pat got fucked up on a ferry boat between Stockholm and Finland and started hurling these mini-sausages at me. I was like, "What are you doing?"

Pat Nowadays, though, we congratulate each other on how little booze we need to get by. You can't be hitting the booze hard and still expect to do your job when you hit your 40s.

Between 1997 and 2006, Cannibal Corpse were forbidden to play songs from their first three albums when playing live shows in Germany. Why? No-one really knows.

Alex Around 1992 or '93 we started hearing from a German politician from the Saarbrücken area. She was from the left side of the German government. We've had ongoing problems there. I believe that this censorship official got the government to put us on a list of stuff that's banned: I believe these laws had originally been created to prevent white power bands from proliferating, because there was a lot of neo-Nazi shit going on after the German reunification.

As far as I recall, music which is "deemed to devalue human life" can be banned, although that's really open to interpretation. My best understanding is that these laws have been used to censor death and black metal bands and also rap acts. Between the late 90s to about 2007, we were not able to play any songs from our first three albums, so there was no 'Hammer Smashed Face', no 'Skull Full Of Maggots' and so on. Usually nobody was at the show enforcing this, but we thought that word might get back to the authorities and we complied with their restriction to be on the safe side. We said, "OK, if this is really the law here, we'll respect it—but we do have to work to get past this." By 2007, and certainly by 2011 when we played Wacken, we were able to play 'Hammer Smashed Face.' We had been given official word that it was OK.

George It's like telling somebody who makes a movie that they can't have a rape scene in it: that scene is part of the movie. Like *I Spit On Your Grave* or *The Accused*. They're totally different movies, but in both cases those scenes are essential parts of the films. Rape isn't right, of course, and we're singing about things that aren't right, but I wish people would see that we're not trying to make fun of those things.

Pat What other lyrics go with this kind of music? It makes total sense. Demented lyrics go with demented music. We never play 'Necropedophile', that's a step too far for me. But what is shocking any more? I see all these terrible crimes on the news. Reality is way more crazy than fiction.

George They say they're doing this to protect their children. They're fucking liars, because they're not. Every crusade starts with the right intentions, but then it gets lost among people's fears about being wrong and losing. That's what's happening in Germany. One year one thing is forbidden, the next year another thing is forbidden. It's ridiculous.

They should talk to the kids and see what they're thinking. Then look at the statistics, whether kids have criminal records and so on. These things are never discussed, even in the US. They should do a survey, like "Do you like Marilyn Manson? Do you like Cannibal Corpse? Do you like Slipknot? Do you like Slayer?" "OK, have you ever been to jail? Have you ever committed a crime?" When you break all this down, you'll really see what effect all this is having. If you're just going to say "Cannibal Corpse is a bad influence," I'll say "Let me see the statistics of death metal fans who are in jail." But they won't do that, because then they'll get answers which they don't want. It doesn't help their agenda. Bob Dole used music for his agenda, and he lost. Where's he at now?

The touring and album cycles continued relentlessly towards the end of the 1990s, with Cannibal Corpse now apparently unstoppable in spite of petty obstacles such as the

German ban. *Gallery of Suicide* was releasd on April 21, 1998; *Bloodthirst* followed on October 19, 1999. The list of bands with which Cannibal had toured was now a who's who of extreme metal.

George We did this tour in 2000 with an insane line-up: Immortal, Deicide, us, Marduk, Hate Eternal, Dark Funeral and Vader. A couple of crazy things happened on that tour. Ahriman from Dark Funeral came up to me and said, "Tonight George, in your honour, there will be a "gay pit"—all naked men covered in sperm." I laughed my ass off. Then he upgraded it to a "gay train." He said, "It will be a line of men with cocks in each other's asses."

The next day I'm singing a song—I'm pretty sure it was 'Covered in Sores'—and I see fucking Ahriman and Matte from Dark Funeral, Tobias and Urban from Vomitory, Legion from Marduk and our tour manager, all with their pants down by their ankles, pretending to be the gay train! I was like "What the fuck, man?" They all shuffle off and turn around, holding each other's hands—and then they leave, except Legion, who obviously thinks "Fuck it," takes his underwear off, strikes a Chippendale pose and does a cock swing at me.

On September 19, 2000, the live album *Live Cannibalism* was released, produced by Colin Richardson.

Pat Colin was easy to work with. He's really interesting, the way he works, and the end result was fucking amazing. His true strength is his ear, no doubt about it. Alex was adamant about not fixing any guitar solos afterwards, so there's some errors on it, but they're supposed to be there—so it's cool.

Surreally, Cannibal Corpse played before Hollywood royalty this year.

Alex Elijah Blue Allman, Cher's son, plays in a band called Deadsy, and he said, "I want you to come out to the Viper Room and show all my Hollywood friends what death metal's all about." It was for a birthday party which he was having. It was crazy: we went over to Cher's house in Malibu, where we hung out and had barbecue, and she

was really nice to us. All these famous people were at the show—Cameron Diaz was throwing the horns!

Tours in 2001 included American and Canadian dates with Dimmu Borgir, Lamb of God and the Haunted, before a European run with a mighty line-up featuring Kreator, Krisiun, Marduk, Nile, Dark Funeral and Vomitory. *Gore Obsessed* followed on February 26, 2002.

Pat Neil Kernon produced *Gore Obsessed*, and I was looking forward to working with him because I'd worked with him in Nevermore. He's a great producer, very open-minded about a lot of things and he wants to stay current. He did a lot of great albums in the 80s with Judas Priest and Queensryche and Dokken, a whole bunch of bands.

Alex The song 'Grotesque' appears on *Gore Obsessed* and it alternates between a diminished scale and a whole-tone scale throughout, so it sounds pretty weird. To me, the scariest music is the music that sounds a little bit unnatural. To try and capture a surreal, unnatural, otherworldly feel, with music alone, you can try odd meters and symmetrical scales. These are ways of being in key but not completely, because things happen in those scales which are strange. Combine weird rhythms and weird scales and you start to create a disturbing atmosphere. You can make scary music that is in key, don't get me wrong, but to go out of key and do odd things with time signatures and syncopation can really produce an unnatural sound: like a band of demons instead of a band of people!

In 2003 the *Worm Infested* EP, made up of leftover material from the *Gore Obsessed* album, and an anniversary package titled *15 Year Killing Spree* both appeared. The following year, Jack Owen quit Cannibal in order to spend more time on another band called Adrift, although he joined fellow death metallers Deicide in 2005. His temporary replacement was Origin guitarist Jeremy Turner, who made way for the returning Rob Barrett in time for the release of *The Wretched Spawn*.

Pat Jack told everyone in the band he was leaving, except me! He was an original member, which isn't great. Jeremy Turner came and filled in, but he had a family and a job in Kansas and we would have had to uproot him if he joined the band. He did a great job though, he really did. Rob reached out to me and I told the other guys we should consider him for the sake of continuity.

I hate member changes, they're never good: from an outsider's perspective, it's a change in the band. So Rob came back and I think it suited him better this time, now that I was in the band and we had a slightly different direction, which he also wanted to go in. It made sense because he'd already been in the band before and he lived in Tampa.

One of Cannibal Corpse's most highly-regarded albums was *Kill*, released on March 21, 2006 and produced by Hate Eternal guitarist Erik Rutan.

Pat Erik's a ball-buster. He makes you do everything over and over, which is a pain in the ass at the time, but at the end of the day it sounds really good. He's one of the best guitarists around too, there's no denying that.

Kill turned out really amazing. Rob's writing was killer. For me personally, this is the best line-up now. We're more focused as a band, and the last three albums we've done with Rutan have been great. Rob and I are totally on the page together as guitarists.

In 2007 a hefty triple-DVD set called *Centuries Of Torment* was assembled for release the following year, Cannibal's 20th anniversary. Its central feature was an epic documentary covering the entire history of the band, filmed by Denise Korycki. A new album, *Evisceration Plague*, was produced by Rutan once more and released on February 3, 2009. A DVD, *Global Evisceration*, followed the next month.

Pete Robertson (tour manager) There was a corpsepaint party at the Mayhem tour in 2009, thrown by Behemoth. At a few given cities where it was only a short drive for the bands, they would hold a barbecue, sponsored by one of the bands. You could do whatever you wanted and the production would throw in a few hundred dollars so you could do something cool. Behemoth decided they were going to do a corpsepaint party in this giant fenced-in area where the parking was. They set up in front of their bus with a couple of hundred dollars' worth of make-up and one by one we all went over there and Nergal, their singer, sat down and did your corpsepaint for you. After a while there were 50 or 60 people all partying wearing this stuff, drinking and hanging out.

George I was the only one from Cannibal who did it.

Alex The rest of us are stick-in-the-muds. That stuff is a pain in the ass to clean off!

George I went to Behemoth's bus and they had about eight gallons of vodka there. I said to Nergal, "This means a lot to me. It really does, so it needs to be really fuckin' evil. I don't care what you do as long as there's an inverted cross on my forehead." He put his hand on my shoulder and said, "You vill be my masterpiece!" I had to get a new passport photo the next day, and the fake blood that I used wouldn't come off my lips. So I've got really red lips in my passport photo... God Forbid had a ghetto-themed barbecue the next night, with do-rags and big chains, with fake diamonds around people's necks.

Pete I made two full bins' worth of a mixture of vodka, sweet tea and lemonade. It was incredibly strong. After two or three cups of it, people were saying, "What the fuck is this?" because they were drunk out of their minds.

Alex That was one of the biggest metal tours ever in the United States. Slayer and Marilyn Manson played the main stage. Our stage at the 2009 Mayhem was one of the heaviest ever: we headlined, and then there was Behemoth, Black Dahlia Murder and Job For A Cowboy rotating, and Whitechapel opening. We were the slowest band on the stage in terms of blastbeats—and we obviously play fast, so you can imagine how fast the others were.

Tours in 2010 continued to spread Cannibal's message...

Alex We did a tour with a band called Devourment, based out of Forth Worth and

Dallas, a really excellent brutal death metal band. We did a couple of shows with them in early 2010 and then we toured with them, Dying Fetus and Vital Remains in the US later that year. It was the last tour of the States we did on that album cycle. I stayed in touch with Devourment's guitar player, Ruben Rosas, on Facebook: he is an old-school metalhead from way back and somehow we got talking about Dimebag. He told me that he had been the guy who introduced our music to Dime when they had been driving around Dallas. He was the guy that Dime told me about in Germany in 1992!

In 2011, before Cannibal embarked on a new album, *Torture*, Pat O'Brien received a startling phone call. The veteran thrash metal band Slayer, short of a guitarist as their axeman Gary Holt was touring with his other band Exodus, were looking to the death metal scene for assistance.

Pat In 2011, Brian Slagel called me and asked if I'd be interested in helping Slayer out. I said sure, and that he should get back to me and let me know. He never called back, so I assumed they'd got somebody else. I didn't think any more of it until I suddenly got a phone call from Slayer's management, saying that they needed me in Madrid in three days! They gave me a list of songs, but it was the wrong one and I ended up learning a couple of the wrong songs. I did the best I could to learn them in three days, checking on Youtube to make sure I knew which solos were whose.

I flew into Madrid and they picked me up and took me to the hotel. I was totally jetlagged and exhausted, but an hour later I was told to be in the lobby ready for soundcheck. I needed another day to prepare, so I think they were a little worried, but it came together and it worked out.

It was stressful, knowing that the whole metal community was watching. The gigs were intense for that reason. There wasn't really time to enjoy the shows, although I wanted to—and in fact I did start to enjoy myself towards the end. All the guys in the band are great, and they're one of my favorite bands, but when you get in that situation all you think about is what you have to do to make it happen.

I'm a perfectionist, so I think I could have done a better job if it hadn't come and gone so fast. I made a few errors: there's a part when Kerry King's guitar went out in the middle of 'Dead Skin Mask' and I couldn't hear him come in, and then I came in wrong so it was all fucking whacked-out. That annoyed the shit out of me. There was another part when I came into 'War Ensemble' a little early, but I was able to come back in so it wasn't a total train wreck. I should have just turned my guitar off and said 'I broke a string!' Afterwards, I did quite a bit of drinking with Kerry King. You can't tell when he's drunk, though: he handles it very well.

In 2012 Cannibal's twelfth album, the utterly brutal Torture, was released. The last of Cannibal's Erik Rutan-produced trilogy, it was globally acclaimed: the sound of a band at its peak.

Rob I might read about a true event and, without revealing what it's really about, base a song on it. Like when I wrote 'Caged... Contorted' for *Torture*, I was reading about the La Laurie Mansion in New Orleans. A really evil woman lived in it a long time ago and she used to do sadistic stuff to people. She'd break their bones and do surgery on people and keep them in cages. She'd do all this in the attic, and people would hear screaming. We write songs about subjects that people don't think about too much. I wrote 'Sarcophagic Frenzy', which is about a big group of flesh-eating creatures coming after you, like a fear mechanism which makes you think 'Oh shit, what's happening?' It's like a short film in a song.

Alex I did Brazilian jiu-jitsu for a few years, and one of the things you do in that sport is bend someone's joint backwards to make them give up. That helped inspire the song 'Bent Backwards and Broken' on *The Wretched Spawn*.

George When we played Mayhem in 2012, there were a lot of people there who didn't know who we were. The bill was Slayer, Marilyn Manson, Bullet For My Valentine, All That Remains, Trivium: a lot of big bands. At the first show in California, there were 14,000 people. I said to myself, "I'm gonna show them who we are." When people ask me if I'm intimidated, I say "Fuck no!"

In 2013, more problems in Germany were encountered when the ban on certain of Cannibal's songs, dropped in 2007, was reinstated.

Alex It just started happening again, and nowadays you could get caught more easily because of fans filming you for YouTube. There would be a risk of arrest if we broke the law, and in fact when we recently played Munich they sent down three officials to make sure we weren't selling the wrong T-shirts and playing the wrong songs. They had told us that we couldn't play 'Scourge of Iron' and 'Sarcophagic Frenzy' from the new album, but it seems arbitrary to me: they also told us not to announce the song titles.

Rob I don't know why 'Sarcophagic Frenzy' is banned in Germany: it makes no sense. It's irritating, because the rules change all the time and we don't understand how anybody is benefiting from us not being able to say the titles of our songs. The kids had to show ID to prove they were 18, in order to even see our merchandise. Our merch guy Mike had to hide the T-shirts behind a wall. I think if kids are raised properly they'll be able to separate reality from fantasy and they'll understand that this is just entertainment. The covers are like comic books, pretty much.

In September 2014, this book accompanied the release of a pulverizing new album, A Skeletal Domain, produced by Mark Lewis. It was classic Cannibal Corpse—relentless and technical, but with atmospherics and textures to complement the bloodletting...

Alex It was great working with Mark. The way he records is very smooth. We had a great time working with Erik on the prevous three records, but we wanted to change things up a little just to keep ourselves challenged, and Mark's system worked really well for us. A Skeletal Domain sounds a little different, not necessarily in the songwriting but in the production. It's just a slightly different style which is hard to explain, because you have to hear it, but every producer—from Scott Burns onward—has given us the heaviest sound they could, but always in a slightly different way. It's cool, because it's a way of making us sound a little different without us changing our style. Pat did more writing than anyone else this time, which is a first for us. His songs are all about heaviness, and the technicality of his songwriting is a means to that end. The first song we released, called 'Sadistic Embodiment', is very fast indeed!

As Cannibal Corpse head into the future, what lies ahead? There appear to be no limits to the band's creativity. Their grim mission will not be stopped easily, it seems.

Alex Music is limitless and I'm not concerned about running out of inspiration. Lyrically, I've found the best way to avoid becoming repetitive is to be very specific about your subject, like a song about a guy who likes to chop off people's heads and arrange them in order in his refrigerator, for example. We've had songs about decapitation before, but not with that angle. So there's plenty of inspiration.

As negative as the material appears to people who aren't familiar with it, the feeling it gives our fans is overwhelmingly positive. I see how much fun people have at the shows: they love the music and they realise that it's a form of entertainment, not instructions about how to live your life.

Paul We want our songs to be good, and we want them to be memorable. Our roots are in classic heavy metal and, although we write brutal music, we want to include melodies too. I'd like people to look back on us as a game-changer: as a band that achieved something. I think the world is a better place with Cannibal Corpse in it.

What is life about, in general? It's about moving forward, and we're building a musical foundation for other bands to use to move forward. It makes me proud, because I feel that I've accomplished something that is worthwhile and positive.

Brian Slagel I would never tell Cannibal that they have to sound a certain way or go in a certain direction, but we'll sit down together when they're rehearsing new material and talk about song titles and where they want to go musically. I'm more of a sounding board for them. I don't tell any of our bands what they should do: it's their art and they should be able to express it, especially a band like Cannibal.

I'm blown away by how long Cannibal's career has been, and also how consistent their music has remained over the years. They've stayed true to themselves and they keep it interesting: they're not just putting crazy song titles out there, they're really taking the music in a different, fresh direction. I'm incredibly impressed by that. A lot of musicians, as they get older, will start going through the motions, and they're not really into it—but the Cannibal guys really practice a lot. It's really important to them to top what they've done before on a musical level, and grow as musicians. That's incredible for a band who have been doing it for so long.

They're the biggest-selling death metal band of all time, due to the fact that they're smart and because they've avoided the problems which their contemporaries have faced. And what's funny is that you'd think they would be pretty weird people, judging by their songs and artwork, but in fact they're the most normal, laid-back, down-to-earth guys ever. You go on their bus and they're super mellow, there's no crazy stuff going on. They're regular people. You tell people that, and they say, "Really?"

Paul We've climbed steadily since day one. We've slowly climbed the ladder and now we're in the best position we've ever been in. This is the longest we've had a solid line-up, and it's all good. We've always been able to maintain our creativity because we've always stayed healthy and because we haven't had to deal with a member being on heroin for five years, or whatever. The five of us together make a band, and it works. That's how we can be around for 25 years and do 13 albums.

Who is Cannibal Corpse? A lot of people might say Alex is Cannibal Corpse, because he's the best bass player in death metal and plays like a machine and writes so much. Others might say it's George, because he's such an incredible frontman and does his job so well up there on stage. But really, we're lucky to have all the guys in this band. We're all good musicians and we're all songwriters, so we all gel together and the band becomes bigger than the members themselves. Our songs stand the test of time.

Pat What we do is very positive. We're a band and we stick to our guns, and most people know that we're writing fiction, apart from a few goofballs who spoil it for everybody and bring censorship on us. It's a good band and we all get along pretty well. I've been in this band 18 years, the longest I've ever been in a band. This is what I want to do with my life and I'm lucky that I'm able to do it. Anybody can make it happen if they try hard enough: we're living proof of that.

Paul I just turned 45. Can I play death metal drums for another 10 years? I think I can. The thing is to sustain the credibility of the band and not become a shell of ourselves, as if our best days are behind us and we're just going through the motions. The goal is to be the best songwriters we can be, the best musicians we can be and the best Cannibal Corpse we can be. If we can do those things, one day we'll look back at our careers and be proud.

Rob We see fans all over the world who collect our stuff and tell us that they gain positivity from coming to see us or listen to us. They tell us that we helped them get through some hard times, which is what music's all about. The lyrics just fill in the blanks in the music: we're not on a mission to change people's lives. Just listen to the music and enjoy it.

Our tours are getting bigger and we have an especially strong following in the States. I'll always want to play guitar and learn about writing songs in different ways. I want all my songs to sound different every time. We have a few songs that we'll never play live because they're just too technical, but we listen to the recordings and say 'That is totally sick!' and feel proud of ourselves. Every album has songs that we'll play live, though.

We've kept our identity. When people hear us they know it's us. But at the same time we've managed not to repeat ourselves. I think we're pretty much at the highest level that death metal is going to go, at least in our era, although maybe another death metal band will come along and prove me wrong.

George Most metalheads know the name Cannibal Corpse, let's not kid ourselves. We totally earned our place. There's no doubt. We paid our dues. I'm not gonna say we're at the top of the metal world, because we're not, but we are at the top of the death metal world. There's still room to climb, and that's what keeps me excited. We're not successful because of all the controversy we've been through. We're successful because we're a great band.

Fuck censorship. We're always gonna be here, and you'll never stop us.

ACKNOWLEDGMENTS

Cannibal Corpse thanks Steve Davis and Chuck Andrews from Good Fight Entertainment, and the relevant publishing companies for permission to reproduce the song lyrics in this book.

GEORGE FISHER

Stacy, Maya and Abigail Fisher, George and Frances Fisher, Chris, Marie and Logan Fisher, Missy, Howard, Miles and Mehki Falcon, Pete Robertson, Brian 'Babyface' Benson, Roger Keene, and all the great crew we've had over the years, Brendon Small, Tommy Blacha, and everyone involved with Metalocalypse, Sam Didier and everyone at Blizzard Ent., Adam D and Killswitch Engage, Shannon Lucas, Ryan Young and Off With Their Heads, Hank III, Alex Story and Cancerslug, Steve Terror and Infernal Majesty, Brian Slagel and everyone at Metal Blade Records, Joel McIver, Erik Rutan, Robin Mazen, Rick and Heather and The Brass Mug, Jack Goodwin, Nick Goodyear, Jesse Jolly and Jay Fossen of Paths Of Possession, Randy Butman, Brian Greer and Jeff Kahn, Dave 'Morgan' Mesa, the Denver Broncos, the Baltimore Orioles, the Washington Capitols and the Washington Wizards (my teams!) and all our fans worldwide.

FUCK THE ALLIANCE!

PAT O'BRIEN

I would like to thank my mom, brothers and the rest of my family, Robin Mazen, Dino Cazares, all my friends everywhere, Brian Slagel, Mike Faley and all at Metal Blade, Nick Storch and the Agency Group, Mesa Boogie, BC Rich Guitars, Ran Guitars, Scott Uchida and everybody at Dunlop, our touring crew, Scooter at Granville Guitars, the Slayer camp and all the fans for their support. Thank you and R.I.P. Michael Trengert.

ROB BARRETT

Maryrose Barrett, Robert Barrett Jr. (R.I.P.), my wife Irina, and all my family and friends. Listing everyone would take several pages, you know who you are! Everyone that we've worked with over the years, and a special thanks to all of our fans around the world for making this whole journey possible.

ALEX WEBSTER

My wife Alison, our families and friends, Joel McIver for doing a killer job with this book, Brian Ames, Metal Blade, Pete Robertson, our crew and everyone else we work with, and most importantly all Cannibal Corpse fans worldwide for making this all possible.

PAUL MAZURKIEWICZ

Thanks to my wife Deana and my daughter Ava for their support and understanding all these years! To my Mom and Dad and my entire family for their never ending support from day one. To all my friends — you know who you are! To Brian Slagel and all at Metal Blade Records, past and present. And to the fans! Without you we would have never made it this far...

JOEL MCIVER

The past and present members of Cannibal Corpse, plus Brian Ames, Randy Blythe, Jim Carrocio, David Ellefson, my agents Lisa Gallagher and Matthew Hamilton, Gene Hoglan, Denise Koricki, Borivoj Krgin, Will Palmer, Ralph Santolla, Brian Slagel, Andy Turner, Alison Webster and the staff of Metal Blade. To my kids: please don't read this until you're 18.

DISCOGRAPHY

ALL RELEASES BY METAL BLADE

EPs

March 23, 1993   Hammer Smashed Face

July 1, 2003   Worm Infested

Studio Albums

August 17, 1990   Eaten Back To Life

July 1, 1991   Butchered At Birth

September 22, 1992   Tomb Of The Mutilated

April 12, 1994   The Bleeding

May 21, 1996   Vile (US Billboard, 151; US Heatseekers, 10)

April 21, 1998   Gallery Of Suicide (US Heatseekers, 22)

October 19, 1999   Bloodthirst (US Heatseekers, 32)

February 26, 2002   Gore Obsessed (US Heatseekers, 28; US Independent 11; Germany, 71)

February 24, 2004   The Wretched Spawn (US Heatseekers, 27; US Independent, 20; France, 136; Germany, 74)

March 21, 2006   Kill (US Billboard, 170; US Heatseekers, 6; US Independent, 16; France, 187; Germany, 59)

February 3, 2009
Eviceration Plague
(US Billboard, 66; US Independent, 6; Austria, 41;
Belgium, 71; Finland, 25; Germany, 42)

March 13, 2012
Torture
(US Billboard, 38; US Independent, 7; Austria, 40;
Belgium, 95; Finland, 35; Germany, 40; Sweden, 37; UK, 126)

September 16, 2014
A Skeletal Domain

Live Albums

September 16, 2000
Live Cannibalism

March 19, 2013
Torturing And Eviscerating Live

November 25, 1997

Monolith Of Death Tour '96-'97 (US chart, 32)

September 16, 2000

Live Cannibalism

July 8, 2008

Centuries Of Torment: The First 20 Years
(US chart, 8; Canada, double platinum)

March 15, 2011

Global Evisceration

November 4, 2003   15 Year Killing Spree

March 19, 2013   Dead Human Collection: 25 Years Of Death Metal

INDEX

All songs and albums are by Cannibal Corpse except where indicated.

ABOUT THE AUTHOR:

Joel McIver is the bestselling author of 25 books on rock and metal. His writing appears in Metal Hammer, Classic Rock, The Guardian and Rolling Stone and he regularly appears on TV and radio.

Info: www.joelmciver.co.uk

Photo by: Andy Knight

CPSIA information can be obtained at www.ICGtesting.com
Printed in the USA
LVOW02s1736060914

402676LV00001B/1/P